Towns a[...]
OF EN[...]

C000261968

TETBURY

Towns and Villages OF ENGLAND

TETBURY

JOHN HUDSON

ALAN SUTTON

Published in the United Kingdom in 1993 by
Alan Sutton Publishing Limited
Phoenix Mill · Far Thrupp · Stroud · Gloucestershire

Published in the United States of America in 1993 by
Alan Sutton Publishing Inc · 83 Washington Street · Dover · NH 03820

British Library Cataloguing in Publication Data

Hudson, John
    Towns and Villages of England: Tetbury
    I. Title
    942.417

ISBN 0-7509-0538-7

Library of Congress Cataloging in Publication Data applied for

Typeset in 11/13 Bembo.
Typesetting and origination by
Alan Sutton Publishing Limited.
Printed and bound in Great Britain by
Hartnolls Ltd, Bodmin, Cornwall.

Contents

Introduction   1

1   Early Days   5

2   The Wool Trade   18

3   The Feoffees   26

4   The Market House   36

5   Church Life   42

6   After the Gold Rush   58

7   Stout Memories   74

Bibliography   84

Index   85

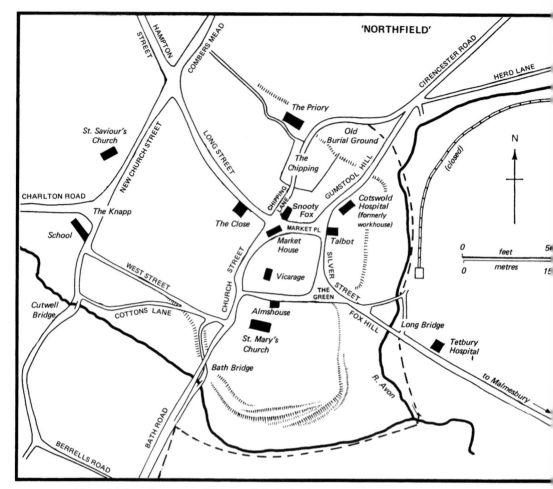

Map of Tetbury (courtesy of Tetbury Civic Society)

Introduction

Not all of Tetbury's history is written in the stone of its streets, but its handsome grey buildings tell us much about its changing fortunes over the past three hundred years. What we see today is a town centre shaped by the community's years as a nationally important market for raw wool, a boom time that lasted from the late seventeenth century until the dawning of the Industrial Revolution, far away up-country, a hundred years later. Tastes in building styles altered dramatically in those hundred years, from the gables, mullioned windows and dripstones of traditional Cotswold architecture to the

Roofscape from the top of the old brewery building, Hampton Street, in 1983

classical revival with which John Wood, his son and others were transforming and making famous Bath, just down the road. Today it is the mixture of these styles, unified by the grey local stone of the south Cotswolds, that contributes so much to the charm of the central streets.

The result is a little town as pleasing as any in Britain, preserved more completely than one might have dared to hope. Some might mourn the fact that the medieval church, apparently as handsome as those of any of the Cotswold wool towns, did not survive the zeal of Georgian churchmen, though the building they left in its place seems scarcely the cause of regret. It is also obvious, to the extent that the old cliché about standing out like a sore thumb has rarely been more aptly applied, that one or two glaring lapses of late twentieth-century taste exist and are known to all who care about the place; but the planners have tightened their net since then, and one must trust that, with vigilance all round, the future is secure.

As for the other great period of change as an expression of self-confidence, the middle and late Victorian years, it was precisely because Tetbury was feeling anything but self-confident at that time that so little was done to sweep away the handiwork of previous generations. It remained the focal point and market-place for vast acres of south Gloucestershire and Wiltshire, and there was still a living to be made from serving the everyday needs of the community. But agriculture, the industry that gave so many families from the outlying villages their daily bread, was

The Royal Oak in Cirencester Road at the turn of the century

sliding into alarming decline. The tale of the drift from the country to the towns was never told more dramatically than in the national censuses of 1891 and 1901, and though Tetbury fared no worse than thousands of other communities up and down the land, it was still a depressing picture. In that decade the number of inhabited houses in the town declined from 969 to 932, and the population slid from 4,386 to 4,157.

So far as wool was concerned, for all of the nineteenth century, Tetburians could only marvel at stories of Leeds and Bradford and their neighbours, all growing vast and prosperous in a trade once deeply enmeshed in the warp and weft of the Cotswolds. These were hellish places, of course, and while they envied the Yorkshiremen their brass, few

Tetbury Carnival, 1909. Phillips the bakers are still very much a part of the town

in Tetbury would have traded the brisk, clear air of the Cotswold tops for the muck of the Pennine valleys. Nevertheless, there was a sense of being left behind, cast aside into a backwater by times running out of control, and that is never good for the self-esteem of a community that has known a degree of prosperity for centuries and a great deal of it until comparatively recent times. What it was good for, as we have discovered, was the preservation of the size and scale of the eighteenth-century town in a way that delights the onlooker today and will continue to do so well into the new millennium.

CHAPTER ONE

Early Days

Even in the Dark Ages, Tetbury was never 'in the middle of nowhere'. Rather, it was a border town, on the verges of Mercia and Wessex, the lands of the Hwicce and the West Saxons. Today, the county boundary of Wiltshire is close to the south-east, and until well into this century it was even closer. The town was also on the ancient highway between Bristol and Oxford, and what enhanced its claim as an obvious place for a settlement was its lofty position above the confluence of two streams, the infant Bristol Avon and a tributary brook. Travel to Tetbury from Cirencester today and the impression is of an upland town on the plateau of the south Cotswolds, its

Bath Bridge in around 1900, with a clear view of the old road down to the packhorse bridge

Malcolm Bristow, antiques dealer and former
monumental mason, restores the Bath Bridge
datestone in 1985

level central streets a natural extension of the previous miles of rolling
countryside. But head into town from Bath or Malmesbury and it is a very
different story, with cottages and terraced gardens spilling down steep hillsides
from the heights of the Market House and the parish church. A site readily
accessible from the west, yet naturally defended against attack from the south
and east. It is no wonder that flint implements of prehistoric times have been
found here, along with Roman coins and other relics of the early centuries
after the birth of Christ. By the time we first encounter Tetbury in written
sources it was already a settlement many centuries old.

'Thirty cassates on the west side of the public street and not far off fifteen
others prope Tettan Monasterium.' In that simple phrase, granting two estates
to Abbot Aldhelm of Malmesbury, King Ethelred of the Mercians gave future
generations of Tetburians proof positive of the derivation of their town's
name: 'Tettan Monasterium' – Tetta's monastery. The year was AD 681, and
that, too, has assumed importance in the local calendar, as we saw during the
1,300th anniversary celebrations of 1981. So who were these distant figures?
Perhaps it is well to determine, first, who they were not. Ethelred of Mercia is
certainly not to be confused with Ethelred I of Wessex, elder brother of
Alfred the Great, who lived some two hundred years later; less still with
Ethelred II of England, the 'Unready' who ruled precariously from 978 to
1016. But this was a realm of saints, as well as kings. Aldhelm was sanctified

Lady with a parasol photographed by F.N. Baxter, parish church organist and choirmaster from 1880 to 1925 and an amateur photographer, who has left us with many memorable views of the town at the turn of the century

after his death, and one contemporary Tetta was the mother of St Guthlac. Another was the abbess of Wimborne, who was a sister of King Ina of Wessex, and she is surely the far more likely candidate. She was the abbess of a monastery that admitted both men and women, with the sexes kept separate, apart from the visit of priests to the nuns for mass. Apparently Tetta saw even this as unacceptable, and barred all men including the bishop from crossing the threshold – the act of a high-born holy woman who feared no one but God. She is also credited by the chronicler Rudolph of Germany with two small miracles.

Rather more prosaically, the 'public street' mentioned in Ethelred's charter is doubtless the Foss Way, the course of which runs north-eastwards on the east side of town, forming the present-day Gloucestershire–Wiltshire boundary and joining the long, straight 'Roman' section of the Tetbury–Cirencester road at Jackaments Bottom, shortly after it has passed through Kemble airfield. The 'thirty cassates' could therefore be assumed to be Long Newnton, which is rated in the Domesday Book of 1086 as thirty hides. As for the fifteen cassates of land near Tetta's monastery, the Tetbury historian Ted Prince estimates that this was enough land to support some fifteen families, perhaps sixty to a hundred people. 'That was a fairly average sized village for this period of English history, and it seems probable to me that their houses clustered round what is now The Green, just to the south and east of the present church,' he writes.

It has a generally favourable south-facing aspect, is well drained and has easy access to water, and probably was surrounded by land which would not have been too difficult to clear for the arable agriculture on which Anglo-Saxon subsistence mainly depended. It was, moreover, a site which was quite defensible, should the need for defence arise. There would also have been land suitable for meadows to the south and west, and plenty of ground for pasture in what was for long known as the North Hayes, and very probably bore that name then. It was also reasonably close, but not too close, to the Foss Way. It was good to be close to what was still in those days an important line of communication. It was bad to be too close to a route that could be used by marauders as well as merchants. In short, it was an almost ideal site for a village in the conditions of those days.

A rather clearer picture emerges of Tetbury at around the time of the Conquest. It was at the centre of a large agricultural estate, already a focal point for its neighbouring hamlets of Upton, Doughton, Elmestree and Charlton. Tetbury and Upton are listed together in the Domesday Book, with seventy-one serfs of various ranks – villeins, bordarers, redsceniters and servi

Elmestree House was enlarged considerably in late Victorian times. Famous names in Tetbury's history associated with the manor include the de St Valery and Sadler families

Doughton Manor was owned by the Talboys family for nearly 200 years between 1628 and 1819, when it passed into the hands of the Pauls of the neighbouring Highgrove

Members of the Baxter family with pets

– plus one priest. Of these seventy-two, fifty-six lived in Tetbury itself – but Domesday listed only heads of families, so it is safe to think in terms of a population in the late eleventh century of around three hundred. William the Conqueror's great survey also tells us that the manor of Tetbury was in the hands of Roger de Lurci, while it had been owned by Siward in the reign of Edward the Confessor, the king who had ruled to within months of the Battle of Hastings before being deposed by his son Harold. Roger de Lurci also held Upton manor in place of the Saxon Aluricus – and in truth, the 4,570 acres over which he held sway in these two manors were but a small part of his lands, for he owned further vast estates in the south of England. He had come over with the Conqueror, and was apparently close to him in the guise of his cupbearer. There is no reason to suppose that Roger saw much of these western possessions of his, since his political interests doubtless centred around the royal court, but one cannot imagine that William's cronies would have been allotted estates that did not add up to something in terms of income and prosperity. If we are looking for proof that this was good agricultural land, its accession by Roger de Lurci is surely it. Not that his predecessor, Siward, was any slouch, for we can only presume he was the Siward, Earl of Northumberland – 'Old Siward' in Shakespeare's *Macbeth* – who came to Edward the Confessor's aid at Gloucester in 1051 after Earl Godwin had raised his banner of revolt against the king at Longtree, just outside Tetbury.

Lasborough Park, a James Wyatt building of 1794, was built for Edmund Estcourt. The neighbouring Lasborough Manor dates from nearly 200 years earlier, *c.* 1610, and was the home of Sir Thomas Estcourt

What we do know, beyond reasonable doubt, is that neither Roger de Lurci nor any other overlord, before or since, put up any great stone castle on that lofty spot that commands the countryside to the south-east of the town. The ancient earthworks described on modern Ordnance Survey maps as a ring and bailey have yielded evidence enough that the Britons had a camp here and the Romans also occupied this eyrie overlooking their strategically vital Foss Way. Yet try as one might, one can find nothing to support the popular view, held by many local people until comparatively recent times, that a mighty keep once towered above these gentle pastures. A number of historians give us tantalizing hints, while delivering nothing in the way of evidence. In Henry VIII's time the king's chaplain and librarian John Leland toured England for nearly a decade, collecting manuscripts and antiquities and leaving towns the length and breadth of the land with pretty little phrases to quote. 'Tetbyri castelle . . . is apon a cliv with doble diches . . . It is now overgrown with trees and busshes of juniper,' he wrote. But Leland was the classic day visitor, the outsider looking in, and we take his words as proof of a substantial structure at our peril. Later that century William Camden, in his *Britannia* of 1586, told a splendid tale of Malmutius Dunwallo, the Britons' first crowned king, building castles at Lacock, Malmesbury and Tetbury, the latter of which 'he called Caire Baldwine and walled it round about 2,000 years since'. Caire meaning 'walled city'? No, caire meaning just any old camp or stronghold, be it of stone, earth or timber, according to Samuel

Farmer Dennis Price with helpers at haymaking time

Rudder in *A New History of Gloucestershire*, published in 1779. Rudder was forthright in his views, setting out consciously to produce an account of the county very different from Sir Robert Atkyns' *The Ancient and Present State of Glostershire of 1712*. 'The same has happened respecting the camps called castles on the heights of Saintbury, Titherington, Horton and several other places in this county where the inhabitants fancy that castles once stood, notwithstanding that it is very certain that there was never any such thing at either [sic] of those places,' he wrote with seen-it-all-before disdain. What made Tetbury particularly topical to him was the fact that the present parish church was being built while he was researching his book, and there had been much excitement locally over the discovery of dressed stone in the demolished medieval building's inner fabric. There had long been talk of the medieval church having been built from the ruins of the old castle, and surely this was strong corroborative evidence? Rudder would have none of it. 'It seems probable, from many circumstances, that there was an ancient house on this spot belonging to the Breuses or Mowbrays, who were the lords of the manor, and that these were some of its remains', he wrote. 'It is not unlikely that some of the stones of the building were used in the walls of the tower, upon which the Mowbray arms are now to be seen.' That verdict of Rudder

Time to gossip on Cutwell Hill, *c.* 1905

is more than two hundred years old, and though many have continued to question it, no evidence to challenge it has emerged in the intervening years.

That having been said, there have doubtless been times when a solid fortress would have stood royal visitors to the town in good stead. Tetbury finds a footnote in the history of the civil wars of both the twelfth and seventeenth centuries, though in both instances a more lively focal point of operations was Beverston Castle, to the west. In 1144, in the depths of the fourteen-year war between King Stephen and his cousin Matilda that reduced the country to anarchy, the royal army set up camp in the town between relieving Malmesbury, which had been besieged by Matilda's champion Robert of Gloucester, and in turn besieging Beverston. This was an earlier Beverston Castle than the splendid thirteenth-century remains that now stand, along with later additions, amid one of south Gloucestershire's most

Beverston Castle and church, July 1909

charming private gardens. But if the medieval walls of Beverston now look rather like one of the ruins that Cromwell knocked about a bit, so they were, for the castle was twice besieged by Colonel Massey's Roundheads. Tetbury was of some significance to the Royalists as a southern buffer against the textile communities of the Stroud valleys, where rugged nonconformity ruled then as it does today, and Parliamentary sympathies were strong. Charles I dined in Tetbury on 8 August 1643, while riding from Bristol to Gloucester, and issued an order to his colonels and other officers to spare the town, but early in 1644 a detachment of Roundhead horse soldiers made light work of dispersing a Royalist garrison in Tetbury, putting the governor Horatio Cary's troops to flight, killing fourteen of his men and taking many prisoners. Massey's troops' first attempt on Beverston after this success was not so fruitful, and they were forced to withdraw after fierce fighting. But their day came some time later when the Royalist governor of the castle, Colonel Oglethorpe, was captured with six of his men while 'in a private house courting his mistress'; the house in question was quite possibly Chavenage, just a mile or so away. Apart from being seen as a triumph of puritanism over

Silver Street at its junction with The Green, *c.* 1890. At the top of the hill is the Crown on Gumstool Hill

loose living, the incident gave the wily Massey his trump card, bargaining with Oglethorpe's deputy for the Royalists to surrender and go free, so long as they left their 'arms, ammunition, bag and baggage' in the castle. Most of the escapees again fell foul of the Roundheads at Malmesbury a few days later, and that was the end of serious Royalist resistance in this part of Gloucestershire. After Charles I had led seven thousand mounted troops and foot soldiers past Beverston from Gloucester to Bath on 14 July 1644, no more was heard of the clash of swords or the roar of cannons.

Even in peacetime, no town on a busy highway goes without its royal visitors, and that was the case in Tetbury centuries before the present Prince of Wales bought Highgrove House at Doughton, about a mile west of town on the Bath road, in 1980. Edward I passed through on his way from Bristol to Woodstock in 1293. Charles II in 1664 and James II in 1687 both paid fleeting visits on their way to Bath, a reminder of the significance of the city a century before its eighteenth-century blossoming. It was Queen Anne's turn

Clark's stationery shop, on the corner of Church Street and Long Street

to be seen in 1702, the year of her accession; she made a longer stay in Cirencester, but this did not prevent the Tetbury Feoffees, of whom far more later, from paying the bell-ringers £1 for their services 'when her Majesty came through the town'. One presumes they had to pull loud and long for such a handsome sum. Not all visitors, however, were so distinguished. The fairs and markets of Merrie England could be lively to a fault, and a few heads were cracked in 1305 when Thomas and Maurice de Berkeley and their henchmen attacked some of their more troublesome tenants who were enjoying a day out in the country from Redcliffe, in the teeming heart of Bristol. Centuries later, in 1683, Tetbury found itself swamped by Scottish pedlars, all of them apparently on the run from the law in Wiltshire and feeling smug and safe on the right side of the Gloucestershire boundary. Trippers from Bristol in 1305, Scotsmen roaming the highways and byways in 1683; incidents such as these, plucked from time, are a reminder of how mobile the population could be, at times when the odds were stacked heavily against long-distance travel, the Foss Way or no. They also tell us something

Feoffees Douglas Goulding and Sid
Mosdell in January 1988, when the
Market House's damaged dolphin
weathervane was taken down for repair

about Tetbury's importance as a market and trading centre, a status it enjoyed
through the three hundred years and more between the visits of the
Bristolians and the Scots, and for further centuries before and after those
bothersome events. Two dolphins leap playfully on this land-locked town's
coat of arms, a great deal more incongruously than they do on that of seaside
Brighton. Why they were never replaced by fleeces and woolsacks is one of
life's mysteries, for never was a town more shaped by a trade than was Tetbury
by the buying and selling of wool.

CHAPTER TWO

The Wool Trade

In medieval times the wool trade was one of the great buttresses of the English economy, and the Cotswold hills were its focal point – not simply for producing the raw material through the splendid sheep breed most usually known as the 'Cotswold Lion', but for marketing it to the rest of Europe. By the end of the twelfth century the great monastic estates of Gloucester, Winchcombe and Cirencester were visited regularly by Flemish and Italian merchants – the Lombards. And the north Cotswold towns of Chipping

The annual woolsack race on Gumstool Hill, a modern introduction that reflects the town's long association with the woollen trade

Charlie Jones, haulier and licensee of the Royal Oak, stands beside a trailer full of sacks hauled by his steam traction engine *King Edward*

Campden and Northleach, and Fairford to the east, were well accustomed to the chatter of foreign tongues as deals were struck to bear the treasured fleeces away along the well-worn pack routes to Sandwich, Bristol and Southampton. That Tetbury was a significant player in this game is not in doubt, though the medieval wool trade here is not particularly well or colourfully documented. Neither, as we have noted, did the town's 'wool church' survive the eighteenth century, robbing it of a monument to Middle Ages prosperity and devotion of the type now cherished by the likes of Campden, Northleach and Fairford. What is more likely is that Tetbury grew in importance more gradually than its northern neighbours, being held in high regard in Tudor times and flourishing mightily in the last century of the pre-industrial age. The reasons for this slow growth are not hard to determine. In the very earliest days, the markets were where the sheep were, and the chilly, sweeping north Cotswold uplands where the canny monks ran their flocks were always seen as the natural habitat of the 'Lions'. Communications and the market were not yet sophisticated enough to save the buyers from Continental Europe the journey almost to the very field in which the fleeces were produced, whereas by Tudor times the trend was towards more centralized selling places; Tetbury, with the Cotswold flocks to one side of it and the busy port of Bristol to the other, could scarcely have been better placed to take advantage of this development.

It was around the year 1200 that the lord of the manor, William de Breuse, granted a charter relaxing many of the feudal customs and regulations of the time and thus paved the way for Tetbury to become a centre of commerce. William was lord for probably only a short while, from some time before 1197 to 1208, but little in Tetbury's early history compares in importance with his decision to encourage merchants to flourish and turn his village into a prosperous little market town. The last we heard of the manor, at the time of the Domesday survey of 1086, it had been in the hands of Roger de Lurci. Since that time it had passed back to the Crown and subsequently been acquired by the de St Valery family, into which de Breuse had married. William fell foul of King John, a common hazard among landowners, though no less uncomfortable for that, and in 1208 the king confiscated the manor from him. In 1219, however, the de Breuses returned in the form of William's son Reginald, and stayed in Tetbury until the estate passed by marriage to the Berkeleys in the late 1400s.

Tetbury tailors and dressmakers, 1909

The first indication of active trading comes in 1221, when there is a record of the existence of two wine merchants – a coincidence that will amuse present-day Tetburians, since the battle for the wine-buyers' pound between rival merchants has rarely been more intense than at the present day. By the mid-1200s the town's market was well established, for farm produce if not for wool, and by 1296 it and the fairs were producing annual tolls of £11 10s., a reasonably substantial sum. Wool was certainly a telling factor in the later years of the thirteenth century, seventy or eighty years on from William de Breuse's charter, and there is documentary proof that Tetbury fair was a recognized wool mart by 1306. Among traders in the town by that time were weavers, tailors, mercers and a draper, as well as shoemakers, tanners, smiths, butchers, bakers and brewers. More unusual callings recorded during the thirteenth century were those of a garlic-monger, a fisherman and a spicer, all of whom were apparently men of some substance. Once again the evidence, here, is of a town with some degree of sophistication, and the income to support such tastes.

Though Tetbury's golden age as a wool town was undoubtedly the hundred years from the late seventeenth to late eighteenth century, it is clear that it was flourishing in Tudor and Stuart times. Around 1545 it was described as one of the best wool and yarn markets in the county; in 1594, in his

Members of the Warn brewing family, *c.* 1920

Survey of the Manor of Tetbury, John Hexham saw the town as 'the third place in precedent among the towns in Gloucestershire', though other observers might well have challenged that claim; and by 1622, with annual tolls up to £120 a year, the market was said to be 'inferior to none in England'. The specifics of these claims made in the mists of time might not stand up to scientific scrutiny, but what can be fairly assumed is that Tetbury was feeling pretty good about itself long before the boom years that shaped the town that we know today. By the early seventeenth century, too, workers in the cottage industry woollen trades that inevitably grew up alongside the market, were beginning to make a real impact on the local economy. It is known that there were weavers and dyers in town from at least the fourteenth century, but by 1608 no fewer than thirty-four weavers were listed among Tetbury's 116 tradesmen, along with nine clothiers, thirteen tailors, six glovers, five mercers, a tucker, a draper and a hatter. More will be said in due course about the height of the town's trading fame, and the part played in it by those two local government bodies perhaps unique to Tetbury, the Feoffees and the Thirteen. But it is interesting to note that when woollen sales were at their peak – in the 1730s quantities of wool and textiles brought for sale were so great that an alternative selling place to the market house had to be sought – there was also a burgeoning market in cheese from North Wiltshire and the Vale of Gloucester and locally produced bacon. Profits from tolls told the story of the decline of both markets, textile and produce. In 1741 they were £52 and £54 respectively, in 1777, £30 and £30, and in 1801, £21 and £10. These are hardly impressive figures, and a sad little account in the *Modern Universal British Traveller*, written in 1779 by an impartial observer with no vested interest in the town, tells its own story:

> Tetbury is a tolerable good town, pleasantly situated on a rising ground. The houses in general are neat and handsome, but there is a great scarcity of water, the inhabitants being obliged to fetch it from wells and brooks at a considerable distance. The market house is in a good situation, and great quantities of yarn are sold at it weekly by the poor people who, in return, take wool and such necessaries as they are in want of.

That scarcely paints a picture of a vibrant community, the textile trade, at least in the view of this witness, being firmly assigned to 'the poor people'. Perhaps not all of them were as poverty-stricken as they appeared – but the account hit the nail firmly on the head when it noted Tetbury's troubles with water supply. An abundance of water was a prime factor in the Pennine valleys becoming the cradle of the Industrial Revolution, but even before that quantum leap, the absence of streams powerful enough to drive fulling mills had seen the emphasis of woollen manufacture in Gloucestershire swing away

A busy scene at the station in Edwardian times

Haulier F.W. Wright's steam wagon, in the days when telephone numbers had two digits – in this case, Tetbury 77

from the upland towns to the moist Stroud valleys. Water retention was a problem in many parts of the Cotswolds – a fact perhaps most spectacularly demonstrated in upland stretches of the ill-fated Thames and Severn Canal – but few communities suffered more miserably than Tetbury. 'The town stands on a hill, for which reason the inhabitants are at a great charge for water in a dry summer,' Sir Robert Atkyns wrote in his great history of 1712. Two years later in his *History of Gloucestershire*, Abel Wantner, who married into the family of a Tetbury doctor and had evidently heard many a tale of woe over the Sunday tea table, addressed the problem in rather more detail:

> The greatest of their wants is water, which in the summer time they are constrained to fetch from as far as Wilton Bridge, near a mile out of town. On the north side of the town (beyond the Chipping) there is a spring whose water within forty paces of its first rise is of such a petrifying nature that covereth sticks and shells over with a strong substance.

Eighteenth-century gentlemen were great lovers of natural curiosities, and Wantner was by no means alone in being intrigued by Magdalen Meadow spring.

Brian Kimber of the town's civic society seen in 1979 after the restoration of the Magdalen Meadow petrifying spring

By the early nineteenth century, even the most dogged optimist was forced to accept that Tetbury's decline as a wool town was terminal. By 1811, the total market tolls were reduced to around £14 for the year, and by 1822 there were just three wool staplers in town, compared with fifteen just thirty years previously. In 1820 *The Topographical and Statistical Description of the County of Gloucester* must have struck a false note with many hard-pressed Tetburians when it noted: 'The inhabitants of this town are principally engaged in the woollen manufactory and sale of yarn, which is sold on the market day in the market house in the middle of the town; whereas cheese, bacon and other commodities are sold in great quantities at a smaller market house.' That smacks of having been written within half a mile of Gloucester Cross by someone who had not ventured into the south Cotswolds for a good many years. The historical fact is that the wool and cloth trade had gone from Tetbury completely by the middle of the century, to be replaced by other occupations which sometimes worked tolerably well, at other times less so. There was still a large country community to be served; quite a well-heeled one in some quarters, with the traditional landowners being joined by numbers of successful merchants and professionals from the cities to the south that were becoming increasingly close through improved communications. Yes, there would still be a living to be made through trading in Tetbury, and there would even be true success stories, particularly in the brewing and building trades. But these, by and large, would be strictly local triumphs. The world had moved on, and never again would the town be the significant player it had been in the regional or national economic fields.

CHAPTER THREE

The Feoffees

From the time William de Breuse granted his charter to the townsfolk of Tetbury around the year 1200, the government of the town was no longer the sole preserve of the lord of the manor. We know that a bailiff who administered the borough and market was in office at least from the last years of the fourteenth century, and that two hundred years later the town jury in the manorial court put a choice of three names for the post of bailiff to the lord's steward every Michaelmas, the autumn quarter day. This town body – there was also a 'foreign' jury for the rural areas of the manor – had the further right to appoint lesser officials, constables, meat inspectors, ale tasters and the like; but the shift of true power from the lord to the townspeople was slow, indeed centuries long, and the breakthrough did not come until one of the richest local boys made good, cut through the red tape in a quite spectacular way.

Tetbury-born William Romney, who died in 1611, emulated another Gloucestershire lad, Richard Whittington, in going to London, making his fortune and rising high in the ranks of the city's guilds and corporation. He was an alderman and sheriff of the city and master of the Haberdashers' Company from 1603 to 1604; the year 1603 also saw him knighted at Whitehall. Through his own marriage and those of his two daughters he was at the heart of well-connected city life, while his business dealings were scarcely less impressive. Because of his long links with the Haberdashers' Company, there is an honourable and perfectly credible tradition that he started his commercial life as a lad in the Tetbury textile trade; whether he did or not, it is hard to believe that his choice of occupation in the city was not influenced by the town of his birth.

His most notable achievement was his part in creating the East India Company in 1600. As governor of the Merchant Venturers' Company, he visited the Netherlands in 1598 to open up new markets in wool and cloth, and in the following year he put £200 into a trading mission to the East Indies. Elected deputy governor of the East India Company in 1601 and governor in 1606, he rose as surely in this organization as he did in domestic politics in London. It was not just money talking, either. He could not have risen through the ranks without his acquisition of vast wealth, but through his

Coronation celebrations, 1953

life he retained a venturesome, imaginative streak. Internationally, in 1610, he was one of the subscribers to Henry Hudson's last, fateful voyage to discover a north-west passage to the Pacific; that quest, of course, ended in the mutiny of the crew of the *Discovery* in Hudson Bay in 1611, and the navigator's death after being set adrift in an open boat. The year 1611 also brought the death of Sir William Romney – but on the south Cotswold scene, rather than the icy wastes of north-eastern Canada, his streak of individuality proved far more fruitful.

For some years he had leased the tolls and profits from Tetbury's markets and fairs from Lord Berkeley, and on his death there were still eight years of the agreement to run. In making this arrangement, the lord of the manor could scarcely have imagined that he was sparking a social revolution. While Romney was undeniably 'new money', he had the credentials of an establishment figure through and through, and when the two rubbed shoulders in drawing rooms there was doubtless much in common between the landed aristocrat and the self-made merchant. It was Romney's will that put a whole new complexion on the future running of the town. He left the market lease to the townspeople of Tetbury, specifying that it should be managed by the king's bailiff and twenty other townspeople, Thirteen of whom he named. Thirteen with a capital 'T', for a body of that name exists to this day, still playing a limited but quite definite role in local life. As well as collecting the tolls, this body was instructed to spend the profits in providing for the poor and financing a schoolmaster and a lecturer at church. Anything left over should be used by the king's bailiff,

> the better to maintain and keep hospitality to credit and countenance his place for the well governing of the town, and to keep such servants and officers as shall be needful for the service of the town and for the just and true weighing of wool, yarn and other things.

Students of human nature will perhaps recognize that while Sir William Romney was doubtless a demon businessman, he and those who helped him draw up his will were perhaps not as well versed as they might have been in the ways of their fellow men. Might one not suppose that there was a danger that his legacy, as it stood, gave rather too much licence to one man, the bailiff? As in the late twentieth century, so it was in the early seventeenth. The markets were booming, and after all the charitable work had been paid

Prominent turn-of-the-century resident
Wallace Munday, dressed in golfing garb for
the Tetbury photographer E.T. Lamb

for, there was still a large amount of money at the bailiff's disposal. After the lease left to the town by Sir William had been renewed, it was no time at all before ritualistic mutterings about where the money was going rumbled on into something stronger, and in 1622 an inquisition or public inquiry led to a chancery decree aimed at regulating the management of the fund.

The inquisition's brief was 'to redress the misimployment of lands, goods and stockes of money heretofore given to charitable uses', and those who sat on the panel included some prominent local names: Sir William Sandes, Sir Thomas Estcourt, John Baker DD, Sir George Huntley, John Bridgeman, Thomas Hodges, Nathaniel Coxwell, Robert Stedwell and the Berkeley estate steward John Smyth. There is no evidence of scandalous disclosures. The lease of the profits of the tolls and fairs was granted to John Smyth, who in turn sold it to the townspeople, but the power of the bailiff was restricted by making him more accountable to the dozen men who joined him in a reconstituted Thirteen:

> Twelve of the most gravest and most discreet townsmen should be as Brethren and Assistants to the King's Bailiff of the said town for the time being to assist the said King's Bailiff in the public affairs concerning the town.

'Most gravest and most discreet': a solemn, sober phrase, and if a portrait of that first Thirteen had survived to this day, it would surely have featured a baker's dozen of long-faced greybeards. Fortunately, we have been left a graphic insight into the less formal spirit of those first Jacobean times by one of the principals in this important episode in the town's history, John Smyth. Smyth, who lived in North Nibley, not far from Berkeley Castle and Tetbury, was a barrister who gave a lifetime's service to the Berkeley estate. He also wrote prolifically, from a dutiful history of the Berkeleys, to a roll call of fighting men, to a delightful account of rustic life in south Gloucestershire. The roll call, *Men And Armour For Gloucestershire In 1608*, is interesting enough. At that time Smyth's master, Henry, Lord Berkeley, was the county's lord lieutenant, and the list was drawn up in response to a request from James I for the names of 'all able-bodied and sufficient men in body fit for His Majesty's service'. Of some 160 Tetbury 'possibles', Smyth listed thirty-two weavers, singled out thirteen men with previous military service and denoted 'those men who were of the tallest stature fit to make pikemen, those of middle stature fit to make musketeers, those of a lower stature fit for service with the caliver [small musket], and those of the meanest stature fit for pioneers or of little other use'.

As interesting a glimpse of social history as this is, it does not mirror rural life in the south Cotswolds nearly so vividly as Smyth's *The History Of The*

Hundred Of Berkeley, which devotes much attention to the everyday speech of south Gloucestershire, not least in a hundred proverbs and sayings. These include such gems as: 'Hee that feares every grasse must never pisse in a meadow'; 'A woman, spaniell and a walnut tree, the more they are beaten, better they bee'; and 'A great housekeeper is sure of nothinge for his good cheare, save a great Turd at his gate', on which Smyth reflects: 'I wish this durty proverbe had never prevailed in this hundred, havinge from thence banished the greater halfe of our ancient hospitallity.' He also has a wistful reflection on 'An head that's gray serves not for mayden's play: in which state my constitucion now stands'.

This, then, was the kind of public official who helped shape Tetbury's history at a crucial stage, unencumbered by the prudery of a later age, certainly. 'Grave' and 'discreet', even by the standards of his day? Who is to say?

As well as the bailiff and his twelve good men and true, the decree provided for 'twenty-four of the most discreet townsmen next to the said number of Thirteen' from whom future members of the Thirteen should be elected. It was democracy of a sort, and with the climate of the times working in their favour, the townspeople soon discovered that you did not have to be the landed gentry or the governor of the Merchant Venturers to make a lot of money running markets in Tetbury. In 1633 they were in a position to go to Lord Berkeley through John Smyth and agree to buy from him the manor and borough, the advowson of the vicarage and the commons for a total of £804, some of which they had in hand and the rest they would have to raise. An elaborate bill of sale was drawn up, but the nub of the transaction was that four men were named as the Feoffees, or lords of the manor in trust, and the Tetbury merchants gained a degree of control over their affairs comparable to that enjoyed at that time only by the burgesses of royal boroughs. The four – names written indelibly on the history of the town – were Richard Talboys of Tetbury, gent., a Yorkshire wool trader who lived in Church Street before buying land in Doughton and building the manor there – not Highgrove – in around 1641; John Gastrell of The Grange, Tetbury, gent., whose family owned what is now known as Estcourt Grange for many years; Richard Box of Tetbury, yeoman; and Toby Chapman of Tetbury, clothier. The latter was a churchwarden at the parish church, as most probably also was Box. Other documents made a conscious effort to keep alive the lesser roles of both the Thirteen and the Twenty-four; it is clear that the lessons of the Romney bequest had been learned, and there was now a general acceptance of the safety and accountability of numbers. Since all this acquisition of power was an expensive process, however, the first task was to cut back on some of the more enlightened provisions of Sir William's legacy.

The Cottage Hospital

The spirit of this pruning had much in common with the regime of public spending stringency of the early 1990s. Until the debt was paid, out went free education for the poor: 'Everyone should pay the schoolmaster for such child or children as shall be taught by him, as well inhabitants as strangers.' As for the lectures in the parish church, while the Reverend Mr Edwards had no doubt welcomed this extra source of income, when the axe fell he simply shrugged his shoulders and continued to deliver them 'out of his love for the town'. Some charity bequests to the poor went the same way, common land was ploughed and the rights of commoners were suspended, and while other

Butler and Son's pony cart

charitable causes were maintained, there was a very pragmatic clause to the effect that should the fairs and markets decay, then any or all such payments could be discontinued at the discretion of the Feoffees. Though the old order had been overthrown, the new rules were tailored very much to the aspirations of the incoming ruling classes, the merchants. It worked, too. By 1640 the townsfolk were able to buy for £1,400 the freehold of the markets and fairs, including the Chipping Croft and old Market House in Chipping Street, which had passed into the hands of John Smyth and others from the Berkeley family. As we have seen, Smyth had the common touch, when it suited him, and he was always a popular figure around Tetbury. But it is clear from our limited knowledge of him that his capacity for feathering his nest knew no bounds, and even while clinching this lucrative sale he had written into the agreement that

> as a declaration and testimony to posterity of the love and kindness showed by the said John Smyth for many years past to present to and for the good of the Inhabitants and Burgesses of the Towne of Tetbury, the said John Smyth and the heyres male of his body shall from henceforth att all tymes bee ffree from payment of any tack, toll, pickage and stallage within the said Burrough Towne.

It was determined from the start that the number of Feoffees would be seven – the figure that stands to this day – with the extra members drawn

White aprons and best caps: the Chipping Steps, *c.* 1885

from the ranks of the Thirteen. Lawyers must have grown rich drawing up these convoluted documents – and in truth, their successors found Tetbury a happy hunting ground for decades and centuries to come, for either the Feoffees or their critics were forever going to court over the extent of the ruling body's power. Perhaps it was all too inbred, this off-beat form of local government that had been thrashed out on the townsfolks' very doorsteps. People grumble about centralized power, but in the end maybe they prefer the ground rules to be handed down to them from above rather than drawn up by the butcher, baker and candlestick maker – with the odds apparently stacked in favour of the same old merchant families for generations to come.

Whatever the rights and wrongs, there were constant allegations that the Feoffees were corrupt, that funds were being misappropriated and that the powers of the Thirteen and the Twenty-four had been stripped to such an extent that they were no longer able to perform the monitoring exercises that had at first been envisaged. What exacerbated this particular problem was that more often than not, power was not shared by even seven Feoffees. In 1700 several inhabitants, including John Bliss the vicar, signed a document complaining that there were just three surviving Feoffees, and calling for the re-establishment of the Thirteen and Twenty-four, the new members to be elected with 'the concurrence and consent of the majority of the commonalty'. The Feoffees were urged to admit only Tetbury townspeople to these bodies, and warned that the petitioners would do all in their power to 'hinder the election of all partiall, corrupt and unqualified persons'. This eight-point 'Tetbury Agreement' – if an agreement indeed it was – is a quite remarkable document, steeped in resentment and distrust. Unhappily, it was far from the end of the story, and in the mid-eighteenth century the Feoffees squandered vast quantities of money from the town's last great boom in litigation and counter-litigation.

In 1739, Francis Savage and Samuel Saunders, the only two surviving Feoffees, brought in new members to support their sale of the advowson against the wishes of the majority in town. In the following year their opponents began a Chancery suit, adding to their allegations a misapplication of funds and the neglect of trust property. The case dragged on for nearly twenty years, during which time four of the original six defendants had died, but at the end of it the air had cleared a little. What was plain, when the dust had settled, was that the power of the Feoffees was on the wane. Market tolls were in free-fall, and as the years rolled on into the nineteenth century, central bureaucracy was not about to allow small towns like Tetbury to become islands of self-determination amid a tide of national legislation.

The first curb on the Feoffees' powers came in 1817, when commissioners for paving, lighting and cleaning the streets were appointed by Act of

A scene at the Royal Oak that symbolizes the dual role of Charlie Jones, haulier and publican

Parliament. The Tetbury seven bowed to the inevitable, ceded their right of soil and aided the commissioners' work with a grant of some £400. Tolls by this time were about £100 a year, but in the Regency years between 1811 and 1820 the Feoffees spent other large sums on the enclosure of the Warren or Common (£2,100) and the remodelling of the Market House (£1,000). There was time for one final conflict in the Chancery Court in 1824, when a new generation of advocates swelled their bank balances with the airing of yet another allegation of misapplication of funds, and a plea for the trustees to be brought to account. But by now the heat was out of the debate, and the Feoffees' role became increasingly restricted to their charitable trusts and the management of an ever-decreasing portfolio of properties. A major incursion into their status came in 1888, when their lands were vested in the Official Trustees of Charity Lands, and there have been other changes since then. They still own the Market House or Town Hall, however, along with various open spaces; and with the Thirteen also remaining a part of local life, there is no shortage of Tetburians eager to take their place among the 'lords'.

CHAPTER FOUR

The Market House

For all its Gothic glory, the parish church must take second place, in many observers' view, to the Market House or Town Hall as the building most readily identified with Tetbury. Chipping Campden's tolsey is more charmingly golden, Dursley's more uplifting as one of few gems in a workaday town, Wotton-under-Edge's better equipped for the day to day needs of modern working life. But none of them dominates its town as Tetbury's does, attracts more admiring glances from passing motorists, sets

The Town Hall seen from the Market Place, with Long Street beyond

The Market House, from the Frith postcard series of 1900

more tourists' cameras clicking. As the late David Verey pointed out in his Cotswolds volume of Pevsner's *The Buildings Of England*: 'All roads lead to the Market Place, the town's focal point.' The Market House was built by the Feoffees in 1655, most likely on the site of a less substantial earlier one, and it was designed as the great tolsey for the sale of wool and yarn, as distinct from a smaller hall in Chipping Street that dealt in Tetbury's other great commodities, bacon and cheese. As early as 1799 the Court Leet noted that 'both Market houses and the whipping post require repairing', but the eventual outcome was the demolition of the smaller structure in 1816 and major restoration to the larger in the following year.

As its name implies, the Chipping had been the site of the original medieval stalls; by the end of the first Elizabeth's reign the focal point for markets had switched to the big road junction in the centre of town, though fairs continued to be held on the Chipping. If the Market House impresses today, nearly 350 years on, it is no more than the Feoffees intended. It was built, after all, within a few years of the purchase of the freehold of the

A view of the Market Place, *c.* 1930, which evokes the vintage days of motoring

markets and fairs rights for a massive £1,400, and several buildings were pulled down to make way for it. As has been noted, the Feoffees spent some £1,000 in restoring the Market House in 1817, taking off an upper storey and filling in the Church Street end, but there had been earlier, controversial extensions in 1740, at the height of Tetbury's boom years. A timber construction again standing on pillars, it involved the disruption of the neighbouring shambles, the meat and animal market, and the allegation 'that £300 had been laid out on an unnecessary building adjoining to the Great Market House for private gain' was yet another brickbat thrown at the Feoffees. Though mortared over and tiled with stone, this was obviously a structure not built for posterity, and nothing remains of it today. What have remained more or less intact are the ranks of chubby Tuscan pillars on which the 1655 building stands, though they, too, have seen some changes over the years. At one time the Town Hall housed a fire engine, and it served as the local lock-up until a police station was built in Long Street. Not until 1884, however, when a new police station and magistrates' court was built at the far end of Long Street, did the town's Justices of the Peace cease to sit here every other Wednesday 'at eleven o'clock in the forenoon'. There have also been jollier moments, however, in those upper rooms. A company of comedians put on a show in 1756, at a time when cynics might have said that the Feoffees fitted that description admirably; in 1759 it was a wire dancer, and late last century there was music from brass, string and drum and fife bands.

The town's splendid horse-drawn fire engine

Excellent acts all, no doubt, though for sheer entertainment among visiting showmen it is hard to imagine anyone surpassing Sequah, the Red Indian seller of patent medicines and puller of teeth who plied his trade at the Ormond's Head. When he was performing the latter task, the historian Sid Mosdell notes, a banjo and drum duet would strum and beat away at full pelt to drown the noise.

Pictures of the Town Hall before the 1817 alterations show it as a three-storey building, with three gable-ends in typical Cotswold style along the sides and two at the ends. This extra storey gave it quite prepossessing height and bulk, especially bearing in mind the restricted area into which it had been squeezed, while the gables added an almost domestic touch to what at that time was the hub of commercial life for a wide area. H.J. Massingham, in his *Cotswold Country* of 1937, mistakenly describes the present building as 'an Elizabethan town hall'. Had he seen the original building, he could certainly have been forgiven for dating it at 1555 rather than 1655. What has survived the years has been the custom of topping the Market House, be it two-storey or three, with a bell turret or cupola. It is unmistakably the combination of the bell tower, the gilded dolphin weathervane and the 1887 Golden Jubilee clock faces that stand out as the most eye-catching features of the Market House today, though the down-to-earth would point out that their quirky charms would be as nothing had not £12,000 been spent on roof repairs and

The 'new' police station at the corner of Long Street and London Road, built in 1884 and seen here some twenty years later

other mundane but vital work in the early 1970s. In fact, there has been a great deal of tinkering around with details of the building, with the present cupola roof dating only from the early years of this century. As for the clock faces, we are told that the pre-1817 dials were curious and elaborate affairs carved in oak and with the motto: *Praestant Aeterna Caducis*. This can be translated as 'Eternal things are more important than transitory things', and the Tetbury historian Ted Prince points out that this is a rather elegant and sophisticated adaptation of a phrase from King Ethelred's charter to Abbot Aldhelm, in which the monarch opines that: 'It is fitting that eternal and enduring things should be purchased in exchange for transitory things.' Ted Prince surmises that the author of the revised motto might have been the Tetbury poet John Oldham, a writer admired by Dryden; it might even have been Sir William Romney, or perhaps simply some seventeenth-century vicar. Today, with its far more plain clock dials facing down Long Street and Church Street, the Town Hall still serves for markets and sales, both on the

The Ormond's Head in Long Street, doubling as the Midland Railway goods and parcels office, before the railway came to Tetbury in 1889

ground floor, amid the pillars and flagstones, and in its main upper meeting room. Greengrocery one day, bric-a-brac and paintings by local artists another; the little markets serve the community in a variety of ways, timeless in all but their ever escalating prices.

Apparently timeless, too, is the building's continued use as a meeting place for the Feoffees and the Thirteen, in a room evidently little changed since 1817. It is difficult, today, to see the Market House as the focal point for trade on a scale that transformed the fortunes of the town, and filled it with handsome buildings that still charm us today. No wonder, even with its ill-fated extension, it was said often to be overflowing with bales and textiles, for it seems so small to eyes accustomed to the sight of warehouses the size of several football fields beside motorway junctions. But it is a building full of character, and it is not hard to understand why, whatever its size, it has a special place in the hearts of all Tetburians. And in the little souvenir shops around the town centre, which building adorns the trinkets and tea towels? The Market House, of course.

CHAPTER FIVE

Church Life

Records of Tetta and her monastery in 681, the first traces of Tetbury in written documents, are proof enough of the church's standing in the town's history. We have already discussed this Saxon establishment, but just as well settled in the folklore of the town is the later Cistercian monastery of the twelfth century. It was a branch of the monastery at Kingswood, near Wotton-under-Edge, where an impressive Gothic gatehouse survives, one of the last pieces of monastic building in England before the Dissolution. This, in turn, was a daughter house of Tintern Abbey, an architectural survivor on a far grander scale, and one cannot but wish that Tetbury had some similar lasting monument to the monks' time here. Apart from anything else, it would have saved a great deal of confusion over the exact site of the monastery. Even the meticulous David Verey, writing in 1970, took at face value the claims of the eighteenth-century house The Priory on the Chipping to be the site of the establishment, and identified the very old

Estcourt House early this century

The fishponds at Estcourt, Whitsun, 1907

building with apparently ecclesiastical windows in its grounds as part of the monastic buildings. A recent brochure for the town-centre Close Hotel shifts the focus even more into the heart of town with:

> The fourteenth-century cinquefoil headed light from the Cistercian monastery that originally stood on the site of the Close Hotel is carefully preserved in our walled garden. A prosperous wool merchant built the house over four hundred years ago, on the site of a ruined monastery.

One cannot, of course, be dogmatic, and who can say where the monks might have had various buildings on their lands? But the general consensus

Evening in Estcourt Woods, July 1909

today is that the monastery was most probably settled in the 1140s on the site of Estcourt Grange, for centuries the home of the founding Feoffee John Gastrell's family; a disused churchyard near the house was mentioned in 1248, and part of the kitchen incorporates a fourteenth-century chapel, its piscina still intact. As for the windows of the little building beside The Priory and the Close's medieval masonry, it must be remembered that substantial houses of the Middle Ages did not vary in many of their architectural features from church buildings; the fact is that certainly by the sixteenth century The Priory's site was occupied by a house known as Hickett or Hackett Court, and in the early eighteenth century Atkyns wrote: 'Hackett Court is an old house at the east end of the town, and it is reported to have been the old manor house.' This might well have been a house to replace the one believed to have been on or near the site of the church – the masonry of which, found in the inner fabric of the medieval church, led some townsfolk in the 1770s to believe that they had found proof of a stone castle on Barton Abbots. There was certainly a case for resiting the manor house, for the water supply was so much more reliable at this end of town.

If this scenario is correct, the outbuilding with its twelfth-century windows would not have been a stable for the monastery but an appendage to the manor, possibly its court house. It would be pleasant to think of the monks living here – and wending their way to prayers, from prime to vespers, along

Old people's dinner, 30 December 1946

a subterranean tunnel leading from The Priory site to church. Alas, no trace of this fabled line of communication has been found, either – and bearing in mind the rural isolation of the two Cistercian houses most closely connected with Tetbury, Kingswood and Tintern, it is hard to see why the order should have chosen to build in the heart of a village that was already the central trading point for a widespread rural area. They even found Kingswood, into which they had scarcely settled, too lively a spot in the civil war between Stephen and Matilda, buying land in Hazleton, near Rodmarton, before moving on again to Tetbury and 'a perennial spring which would never fail to supply them with water'.

Religious life was high on the political agenda in those distant times, and the siting of monasteries was a constant preoccupation of the monarch, landowners and Rome. There were years of debate over the relative importance of Tetbury and Kingswood, with the former at one time seeming

The Chipping, *c.* 1905

to have the upper hand, Kingswood being seen as the grange; but in 1149 the monks felt it safe to return to Kingswood, and though we do not know whether they abandoned Tetbury completely at that time, it is clear that the more southern house became the dominant one from then on.

The early history of the parish church is scarcely better defined. We know that the presence of a priest was recorded in the Domesday survey, that the landowning de St Valerys gave the building to the Abbey of Eynsham, Oxfordshire in 1160, and that it stayed in its possession until the Dissolution in 1540. We also know that in 1303 the Bishop of Worcester ordered an inquiry into the conduct of the rector Simon de Prewes, whom he had been told 'neglects his cure of souls and does not serve his church, but consumes its goods on his own pleasures'. Atkyns tells us that the church was large and handsome, with an aisle on the south side and two on the north, while in later years the grammar schoolroom was to be found over the porch on the south side. A mighty tower and steeple were added in the fifteenth century. Both Atkyns and Rudder were happy to record that the church was dedicated to the Blessed Virgin Mary, as it is today, but the Revd Alfred Lee, writing with an intimate knowledge of the town in his Tetbury history of 1857, reflected that since Tetbury Fair was on 22 July, St Mary Magdalen's Day, 'I have no doubt the church was dedicated to that Saint.' What strikes one is

Sunday school outing to Weston-super-Mare, 1913

that by the time Lee was writing, there had been plenty of pragmatic juggling around with public holidays up and down the country, and there could have been all kinds of reasons, from the chance of fairer weather to harvesting considerations, why 22 July had emerged as a more convenient fair day than the Blessed Virgin Mary's 8 September. Be that as it may, there seems no doubt that for centuries the church has been dedicated to the Mother of Christ.

Atkyns noted some interesting monuments in the old church; one of them showed William de Breuse, the grandson of the Conqueror's aide, lying cross-legged in armour with the Crusader's lion at his feet. This did not survive into the new building, possibly because it was in too poor a state of repair, possibly because of over-tidy minds. The face was found some years ago, and astonishingly, other parts of the memorial were rediscovered in the restoration of the early 1990s. Today they are to be seen in the church ambulatories, along with effigies of the Gastrell family and ancient flock masters. Atkyns also admired a 'fair wall piece' in the south porch showing John Savage, gent., kneeling in his sable robes, while in the present church, a joint monument to Sir William Romney and John Wight sent out a blunt message to the fractious townsfolk at the end of the litigious eighteenth century: 'Reader, encourage no unnecessary suits of law amongst thy neighbours, but always follow after the things that make for Peace.'

Medieval churches, for all their splendour, were not always built as soundly as they might have been, and there was alarm in 1662 when the structure was 'extraordinarily shaken by reason of a great tempest'. The situation had become critical by the early eighteenth century, and in 1729 it was agreed to apply to the king for permission to raise funds to enable the vestry to repair

An immaculate wedding group photographed by E.T. Lamb

the chancel and other parts of the church. In a brief of the following year, George II empowered the petitioners to 'ask, collect and receive the alms, benevolence and charitable contributions of all our loving subjects throughout England, Wales and Berwick-upon-Tweed'. The Tweedsiders' response to the Tetbury chancel appeal is not to hand, but in spite of some remarkable responses – 7s. 2½d. collected in Warrington, then Lancashire, 13s. 8d. at St Mary's, Reading – only £400 of the hoped-for £2,600 was realized. There was then general disagreement over what was to be done – to make do and mend or to launch a major drive for a complete rebuilding programme, perhaps by the Feoffees selling the living – and in the unhappy Tetbury tradition of the eighteenth century, the argument did not end until appeals had been made to Parliament and threats of writs had flown around. Those who were keen to rebuild the church reluctantly agreed to allow the £400 to be put to repairs, but only if an independent expert could be brought in to testify that the work was satisfactory. James Gibbs, the prominent architect called in to perform this task, duly descended upon Tetbury with the king's carpenter and a master builder from Oxford in tow. A formidable trio – but the inspection turned to low farce when, after Gibbs's report had proved unfavourable, it was discovered that he had not personally inspected the roof repairs, 'as, indeed, he could not well, being a person in years and very corpulent'. At this point the Lord Chancellor was called in to

Curate Brownlow, an inspiring churchman who spent part of his early ministry in Tetbury

intervene, and a report by the comptroller of the works suggested that a further £400 should be spent before all was well. This never happened, but as the century rolled on, the Revd John Wight, curate in 1740 and vicar from 1741 to 1777, found himself at the head of the campaign to demolish and replace the old church. Wight was a forceful character, taking what he believed to be the wishes of his flock very much to heart, and something of his forthright manner can be seen in a letter to the Lord Chancellor explaining the need for a new church:

> The windows are so much out of repair the people cannot meet together without greatly endangering their health. Some have already contracted violent fits of illness and others, I believe, lost their lives . . . The Bishop's Court is not willing to inter-meddle as the case lies before your Lordship, so that I cannot avoid begging your orders for leave to the churchwardens for repairing the windows to prevent the loss of my congregation. Unless something is done before winter, I am very certain I must not hope to see the tenth part of my people at Church, which is open to the wind almost on every side.

With fears that whatever the outcome of repairs, the old church would still be 'an ugly, inconvenient edifice' – whatever became of Atkyns' large and

John Foster, town crier and beadle

handsome building of only a few decades previously? – Wight and his supporters set about raising funds with a will. The vicar himself gave £700, a sum he probably more than doubled as the years passed by. A house in Church Street was sold for £250, the kind of money older readers might recall spending on their first home in the inter-war years. A society was formed, in which members paid 2s. 6d. if they attended the quarterly meetings – and 3s. if they did not. More than £535 was collected by this means alone, and by 1777 enough had been amassed for the great task to be set under way, with only the tower and spire of the earlier building surviving. One central figure who did not survive to the opening in October 1781 was John Wight, for the vicar died late in the year work on the project began. At least he presumably saw the old building he so detested opened up a little more to the four winds before his demise. The architect and builder for the project was Francis Hiorn of Warwick, and his design was a striking example of early neo-Gothic, a lofty, light and airy place of slender columns and clear glass – and in contrast, dark and bulky box pews. A curious feature was his introduction of ambulatory corridors on three sides, with doors leading to the side aisles: 'More like the Opera House at Covent Garden than anything else', ruminated David Verey, a man who surely knew more about church architecture in Gloucestershire than anyone. Verey was not over-critical of the 'Victorianization' of the church in 1900, but it must be said that many other

Sunday school outing from Tetbury station at around the beginning of the First World War

East comes West: cast members of *Princess Ju Ju*

people were, not least a succession of vicars. In 1971 the Revd Michael Sherwood compiled a church guide based on the work of his predecessor, the Venerable W.S. Llewellyn, and it was a little book that pulled no punches:

> The proper place for the organ is obviously in the gallery in the west end. The recess in the wall was evidently made to house the organ. It was moved to its present position, where it blocks the light from the chancel, in 1900, at the same time as the platform was erected on which the choir stalls now stand. This was done in the pious imitation of the layout of a cathedral, which has done so much damage to our parish churches. It was musically, aesthetically and liturgically unfortunate.

This was part of the background to a major refurbishment of the parish church in the early 1990s, culminating in its rededication in the presence of the Prince of Wales by the former Archbishop of Canterbury, Lord Coggan, on 8 July 1993. A mighty undertaking costing some £500,000, it saw the organ restored to the west gallery from the chancel end of the south wall, the raised chancel removed and the choir, too, placed on high at the west end, the chancel screen of 1917 taken down and the church redecorated throughout in white. The great stained glass east window is now revealed in its full glory; like some other replacement windows of the Victorian era it is not to Hiorn's original specifications, but thankfully there was no move to include it in the purge. One imagines that what has been done – angular votive candle stand, plate metal pulpit, *et al* – has been quite enough to last some of the more traditionalist members of the congregation a lifetime.

The year 1993 also marked the centenary of the church tower and steeple. The fifteenth-century originals had been spared in the rebuilding of 1777, but within a dozen years a note in an old prayer book tells us that 'great thunder and lightning happened by which the parish church, and particularly the steeple, became greatly damaged'. In fact it lasted the best part of a further hundred years, but by late Victorian times it was a curio of the south Cotswolds, leaning eight inches to the east and an amazing 4 ft. 6 in. to the south. Folks came from miles to view this oddity, and could not believe that there was a more spectacular lean to be seen in Chesterfield or Pisa.

While all this might have been good for the tourist trade, it did nothing for the nerves of Vicar Horwood, who was already under constant pressure from the monthly *Tetbury Advertiser*, which had taken a virulent dislike to him. Some members of his flock were rather more positive, however, and as the memorial plaque under the west window tells us, both the tower and spire were rebuilt as a gift from W. Hamilton-Yatman of Highgrove, now the home of the Prince of Wales, in memory of his captain son; it cost some £10,000

The church on the hill, a landmark for miles around Tetbury

and was completed in September, 1893. It is said that the Hamilton–Yatmans expressed the wish that they would be able always to see the tower uninterrupted from the front door of their house. By the same token, there is still a fine view of Highgrove from the top of the tower, as those who have taken advantage of its occasional open days are aware. Not that the Prince of Wales is alone in enjoying a pleasing view of Tetbury parish church. We must stand by our estimate of the Market House as the dominant building in town, and its best-known landmark. But approach Tetbury from many directions and the first you will know of it is that finger soaring to the sky, the tip of the spire just 14 ft short of 200 from the ground. For the surrounding countryside at least, it is St Mary's church that symbolizes the presence and spirit of the town.

Not so many people are aware of St Saviour's church in New Church Street, formerly Cuckold's Knapp, on the other side of town from the parish church and very much on the other side of the metaphorical tracks when it was opened in 1848. It was built quite unashamedly as a little church for the poor, for even after galleries had been added to St Mary's, there were still not enough free pews for those who could not pay for allotted places. One

St Saviour's church was opened in 1848 but is now redundant

problem, of course, was the box pews, uneconomical of space and giving every indication of being very private property, even if they were unoccupied. Indeed, some of them were kept locked when not in use, even if it was standing room only elsewhere. In his history of 1857, the Revd Alfred Lee spelled out the problem as he saw it in 1842, when a new chapel of ease was first mooted:

> At this period, the population of the parish was about three thousand, of whom it was assumed that three-fifths, or upwards of eighteen hundred persons, were poor, as they occupied houses assessed in the rate at a sum not exceeding four pounds. The accommodation for these in the parish church consisted of two hundred and forty sittings only, and these were mostly situated in a most remote part of the church.

The church built to alleviate these problems was certainly no tin hut, but a building giving every impression of a pleasant village church on the outside and finished to a very high specification within. It was designed by S.W. Daukes, an architect best known in Gloucestershire for his Royal Agricultural College at Cirencester, but for the long chancel he employed the

Pugin and Hamilton partnership to paint and gild the reredos and ceiling. Today there is a sound ecumenical movement in Tetbury, with a council of churches representing all the major Christian denominations.

In the 1840s there was an ecumenical spirit in the Church of England alone, for while the vicar, John Frampton, was low church, his curate, Father Charles Lowder, was one of a significant number of Cotswold clerics influenced by John Keble and the Anglo-Catholic Oxford Movement. Father Lowder, a foreceful figure who later became nationally known for his work in London's docklands, was evidently given a full say in the design of St Saviour's, for it was typical of the lovingly-crafted little churches favoured by the Oxford or Tractarian movement in those years when its influence was at its peak. The fact that the low church Daukes was given leave to draw upon the expensive talents of Pugin suggests that even at this early stage of his career, Lowder was not the kind of curate who would quake in the bishop's presence and declare his egg excellent in parts. Anyone wishing to depress himself with allegories of life will find much on which to reflect in the fate of St Saviour's, opened by public demand in 1848, threatened with demolition in 1976 and now kept standing largely by the grace of the Redundant Churches Fund. A town like Tetbury can ill afford to let an amenity such as this go to waste indefinitely; a challenge for the millennium, now that the parish church restoration has been achieved, must be to find a suitable and dignified use for this still consecrated but sadly neglected building.

The old Congregational church, now the place of worship of the Methodists and United Reformed church, built in a corner of The Chipping in 1861

The wider ecumenical spirit has been abroad in Tetbury for some little time, for the town's Roman Catholics occupy a chapel on The Green, now known as St Michael's church, that was first built by strict Calvinistic Baptists in 1872. The sect survived there until 1940 and the Catholics moved in two years later, having first come to the town only in 1935, meeting in a house in Silver Street as a branch of a Salesian community in Malmesbury. The fact that 240 free places at the parish church were deemed so inadequate for the needs of the town that it was felt necessary to build a new church in haste, is made all the more remarkable by our knowledge that at around the same time, mid-nineteenth century, the Baptists had congregations of more than 200, the Independents some 130, Latter-day Saints some 43 and Wesleyans 28. These sects were dotted around various meeting rooms over the centuries, leaving a legacy of little chapels that perhaps suggests that the Nonconformist tradition was even stronger than it appeared. Today their congregations are joined together as the Methodist United Reformed Church, meeting in the Malmesbury architect Thomas S. Lansdown's Romanesque and distinctly un-Cotswold chapel built in a corner of The Chipping for the Congregationalists in 1861.

CHAPTER SIX

After the Gold Rush

In the wake of the demise of the wool markets and the textile trade they fuelled, Tetbury slipped gently and easily in the nineteenth century into the mantle of a quiet little country town in which not a great deal happened. As we have seen from the Revd Alfred Lee's statistics, there was not much money about in the middle of the century, with the clergyman classifying some eighteen hundred of a population of three thousand as poor. There was never any shortage of competition among the inns and beerhouses for what little spare money there was in the men's pockets. Just as the main streets today are dominated by antique shops – 'Another antique shop? That's just what we needed' is the familiar cry when yet another dealer moves into an

Shops at the junction of Church Street and Long Street

empty property and declares his intent – in the eighteenth and nineteenth centuries they were almost shoulder-to-shoulder with places of refreshment.

Tetbury was a convenient and popular coaching stop, so much of the money taken by the larger establishments around the Market Place was the best kind, hard cash from outsiders helping to boost the local economy. Neither was Tetbury unique in having stretches of pavement along which every other business was a pub, or so it seemed; the picture was similar in many other parts of the country, particularly in well established market towns. Nevertheless, the figures of thirty-three inns recorded in 1715, and forty-two licensed victuallers in 1755, a great deal more than one for every ten townsfolk, men, women and children, do seem a little surprising. Then again, so were those church and chapel attendance figures of the middle of the last century. These were different times in so many ways, in social and religious habits but not least in the economics of running a business and a home. Do well selling beer to outsiders on market day, a penny profit here, a ha'penny there, and it would not be long before there was enough in the kitty to keep the family in bread, vegetables and bacon for the week. By 1891 the number of public houses was down to twenty-two, most of the casualties in the intervening years being small side-street meeting places, some of them scarcely stretching beyond a cottage's front room.

The Three Cups opposite the Market House on Church Street, with its three gable-ends, was among the busiest meeting places and leading coaching

Church Street, with the old Three Cups building now occupied by Witchell's ironmongers

The Chipping Steps, *c.* 1905

houses. It was fabled locally as one of the Roundheads' haunts during the siege of Beverston Castle, while there seems reasonable circumstantial evidence that Jane Austen had it in mind in Northanger Abbey when she wrote: 'We drove out of the inn yard at Tetbury when the town clock struck eleven.' In its yards would be kept much of the paraphernalia for the market, stalls and barriers and so on, and being just a few strides away from the Town Hall it was a favourite place for the Court Leet dinners that figured prominently on the town's social calendar. Strangely, it did not begin to survive the demise of the coaching trade in the mid-nineteenth century, and in the 1850s it was turned into an ironmonger's shop and smithy by William Sealey, who later sold it to the Witchell family. It remained in their hands until 1972, when Syd 'Trooper' Witchell died, and in the following year it was demolished as a safety hazard. The building that replaced it revived the gable-end theme, without the architects trying to copy it slavishly – but there are still diehards around who reckon that those old leaning gables were not nearly so fragile as they looked, as the demolition men discovered when they came to slice through the timbers.

Perhaps, today, there might have been a greater effort to preserve what is there. But it cannot be denied that the old Three Cups building was looking far from its best in those later years, and that could equally have been said of much of the town in the first half of the twentieth century. It was low-key, down-at-heel, imbued with a spirit of make-do-and-mend. Small country towns tended to be. People knew one another's business, more or less, so there was little point in showing off to a very restricted world that could see easily through pretensions and overstretched ambitions. So long as the inside of your shop met with your neighbours' expectations of hygiene and efficiency, which in truth were not always exceedingly high, they did not worry too much if your sign and window frames did not get painted more than the odd once in a generation. Even residents who remember Tetbury no further back than the early post-war days of forty years ago speak of a community in which townspeople went out to the shops with the expectation of at least recognizing everyone they saw, and being on nodding terms with most. When they reached the hub of the town they would have a choice of at least three or four well-stocked grocery shops, likewise butchers, bakers, hardware stores and tobacconists. By the time people were becoming

The carnival procession swings into Church Street, 1909

self-conscious about the scruffy old Three Cups building at a prominent corner of town, the new age of antiques and bijou gift shops had already dawned; in a sense, the door had been ajar since the motoring, cycling and hiking boom of the inter-war years had brought to the town increasing numbers of people with nothing but pleasure on their minds and a little money with which to indulge their fancy. By the late 1960s it was a world of more leisure time, more visitors, more money – and since the image of the Cotswolds was always up-market among city dwellers, even if many country-living residents knew differently, it is perhaps no mystery why Tetbury eventually found its niche in the antiques and decorative arts trades.

The White Hart, known to be on the corner of the Market Place from at least 1594, vied with the Three Cups at the top end of the market. Its big breakthrough came in 1852, when it was rebuilt by R.S. Holford of Westonbirt to designs by Lewis Vulliamy. On its first floor was a ballroom for the Beaufort Hunt's social functions, an asset that gave it a cachet enjoyed by

Two famous inns flank the Market House, the White Hart (now the Snooty Fox) on the left and the long-gone Jolly Butchers, far right

The hunt meets outside the Trouble House inn

no other inn in town. It was inevitable that the well-to-do in the country areas would want a watering hole in town suitable to their status, and the hunt's interest in the White Hart came as a godsend at a time when the railways were sweeping the coach routes off the map. Hunt and race balls, smoking concerts, auctions, public meetings addressing the burning issues of the day; every town needed a place like this in Victorian times, and there is no doubt at all that the White Hart filled the bill. Later, in more democratic times, that sprung-floored assembly room served as Tetbury's first picture house, musical accompaniment on violin and piano by the Perretts, father and daughter. The cinema later moved to the converted stables, eventually facing the world as the New Palace, but the 1960s put an end to all that. Far from being the 'swinging sixties', this decade in Tetbury saw off both the railway and the cinema. On the other hand, if both facilities had been better used, it might have been a different story. Not that the Three Cups and the White Hart were the only inns equipped for relatively large-scale gatherings. In 1771, the town assembly was held in the White Lion; in the 1790s a hall known as Cot's Great Room, behind the Angel in Long Street, was used for musical events and balls; and a travelling troupe used the theatre attached to the Prince and Princess in the Market Place in 1815.

Today, the White Hart remains one of the most comfortable and luxurious

Cheerful carnival faces, 1909

hotels in town – albeit under the guise, for the second time in its history, of the Snooty Fox. First dreamed up in the 1960s when the business was bought by Maxwell Joseph of Grand Metropolitan, who had a house almost on the doorstep at Stinchcombe, it is a name that irritates those who are prone to be riled by such change. Its saving grace is that the phrase has a time-honoured country pedigree as a description of old Reynard sniffing the air for scents – and with its Beaufort Hunt connections it could be argued that it has a certain aptness. It must certainly be many a long century since the Duke's hounds chased a white hart over the south Gloucestershire countryside.

The Close is the other major town centre hotel, and extremely luxurious it is these days. The £500,000 restoration of the parish church in 1993 was a reminder of how a large and centuries-old building can soak up the hundreds of thousands of pounds, and one shudders to think what successive owners of The Close have sunk into it in the past twenty years. Internally and externally it is delightful, with its gardens to the rear coming as a revelation to visitors who had not realized that Cotswold town houses that face the world with little more than window boxes or hanging baskets as adornments often back on to grounds that would grace a fair-sized country mansion. They would doubtless be even more surprised to learn that in the case of The Close, the gardens at one time stretched the entire length of the rear of Long Street.

Old Post Office Stores, Prouts Stores; grocers vied with each other in the Long Street of the early years of the century

One of the secrets of The Close's appeal is that for most of its long history it was not a hotel at all, but the residence of some of the town's most wealthy inhabitants – in many people's view, the best house in town. In the wool towns of the Cotswolds it is pleasant to think of streets punctuated by large but fairly unprepossessing looking buildings that, on entry, turn out to be palaces, in the tradition of Florence or Naples. There are parts of Cirencester where that happens – but rarely anywhere else in the area, and certainly not in Tetbury; it has some very fine buildings indeed along and off its major streets, but no other can match the grandeur of The Close.

It was built by John Seede, a property developer who came to the parish in around 1550, and was seen as a 'fayre new building' in 1594. Seede's thrusting and unscrupulous son sold it to Sir Thomas Estcourt, one of the most prominent local landowners of Elizabethan times, and it passed into the hands of another of the top Tetbury families when Francis Savage married Mary, the daughter of Sir Thomas's son Edmund. Later owners were members of the Paul family, giant fish in the not so large pond of the Gloucestershire squirearchy and county set of the eighteenth and nineteenth centuries, and hereby hangs a tale. In the mid-nineteenth century, the solicitor Josiah Tippetts Paul owned medieval property on the east side of The Chipping, and it is known that during renovations an ancient arch, at the very least, ended up in the grounds of The Close. This clearly has some bearing on the belief of some that the house is the site of the twelfth-century Cistercian monastery. Older residents will well recall the final private owner of the house, Lieutenant Colonel E.F. Morrison-Bell. By the time he died, The Close was not in the best of heart, and in 1974 it was seriously damaged by fire. Its progress as a hotel since then, under a variety of owners and not always in the best of economic times, has been quite remarkable.

Another centuries-old coaching inn is the Ormond's Head in Long Street, on the site of what we know were adjoining inns in 1696, the Lamb and the King and Queen. There is an intriguing tale of the landlady at the Lamb being fined for 'suffering indecencies in her house on a Sunday', the singling out of the sabbath suggesting that it must have been acceptable for the other six days of the week. One can think of hotels in other towns where the amalgamation of two pubs has led to some unusual names on the sign – the Swan and Cemetery, Railway and Naturalist, Bull and Royal spring to mind; but it was evidently felt that the King and Queen and Lamb did not quite hit the mark. In choosing to commemorate the Jacobite Duke of Ormonde, the owners at least kept flying a Royalist flag of sorts, even though those who allegedly toasted the Pretender in its bar were scarcely showing conventional loyalty to the Crown. The new name was in use by 1742, and long after its days as a flourishing coaching inn, the Ormond's Head adapted to the new age by becoming a receiving depot for the Midland Railway at Nailsworth.

Pram parade at the carnival, 1909

Mr Rudder the cobbler in Church Street, *c.* 1900

The GWR carrier used the Prince and Princess pub's stables, close to the White Hart on the Market Place, and when it closed in the 1920s the Ives family founded the Tetbury Transport Company on the site. The Tetbury historian Sid Mosdell tells a tale of successive landlords at the Prince and Princess being cursed by misfortune after some customers had roasted a Bible on the taproom fire. The wrongdoers, too, all apparently came to a sticky end. This is also the inn under which the secret passage from the non-existent monastery in The Chipping is said to have run. Altogether, it sounds to have been far too creepy a place in which to relax after a hard day's toil.

The carriers' carts were the lifeblood of the villages surrounding market towns; we tend to think we have never been better provided for with delivery and courier services between A and B, but a century ago places like Tetbury were never without a dusty little office and desk where you could leave a parcel to get to Auntie Nellie in Leighterton by Friday morning. Sherston was served by Goldings Horse Drawn Conveyances. Bendall's was the name for Minchinhampton and Chalford. In later years, some of these country carriers simply bowed to the dawning of another age and hung up their harnesses, while others moved with the times and became some of the most successful hauliers and coach operators in the land.

History does not tell us what the townsfolk had to say when the name

Market Place, with the Prince and Princess pub on the left and the GWR parcel office also prominent

change to the Ormond's Head took place, but many Tetburians can look back a dozen or so years to the day the sign above the door became the Gentyl Gardener. The move was not universally popular. Some even argued, more in hope than expectation, that 'Gentyl' discriminated against Jewish customers, and the old sign should be restored forthwith. That did not wash, but in the years since, the less Chaucerian spelling of the word Gentle has been adopted, and tourists seen lunching in the bar in the summer of 1993 seemed to be enjoying their meals just as much as if the pub had been called the Ormond's Head.

The Eight Bells and the Talbot, houses once as much part of the fabric of the town as the Market House and parish church, have passed away as inns just as surely as the Boot and the Jolly Butchers, the Soldier and the Angel, the Catherine Wheel and the Dolphin and a score or more others. There are the happier sights of old favourites still trading – one hesitates automatically to equate existing with flourishing in these recessionary times – and it is cheering to see the signs still outside the likes of the Crown at the top of

Fire brigade captain, Edwin Webb, at the door of his Talbot Hotel

Prince of Wales regulars could always be relied upon to raise a glass when only happy news came out of Highgrove

Gumstool Hill, which celebrated 300 years of hospitality under various names in 1993; the Royal Oak in the valley below, which reminds us of the tree-climbing monarch Charles I's passing through the town; and the Prince of Wales or 'Drum and Monkey' in West Street, where the regulars could always be persuaded to raise their glasses to toast the birth of the latest little prince when the Press still saw events down the road at Highgrove as a royal fairy story. There has even been a newcomer to buck the trend, the Priory Inn in London Road, a big, modern hotel and restaurant opened in 1980. And as for food, if you wish to take Indian tandoori or Chinese chicken and pineapple home with you, or sit down to Italian pasta or the finest of French dishes, then that is no problem to the caterers of modern Tetbury. It is a great deal more than could be said for the town of 1755, for all its forty-two jolly mine hosts.

It could be said, however, that the present generation is missing out on age-old fun and games. True, there is the annual bank holiday woolsack race up Gumstool Hill, which looks like some ancient torture even though it is not, but where now the Tetbury Races, the bull-baiting and the jeering at old crones in ducking stools? They knew how to make their own 'entertainment' in those days. . . .

Tetbury horses were famous in Tudor times, swift in the chase, and in the

At the top of Gumstool Hill, with Hussey's sanitary plumbers – another vanished name

Richard Tugwell's champion pony Dainty, seen on The Green in 1903 before being sold to a breeder in America

A busy scene not so long ago: the cattle market at the bottom of Gumstool Hill in 1978

British Museum a valuation of the property of Robert Dudley, Earl of Leicester, after his death in 1588 shows among his six horses a Bay Tedburie, a Bald Tedburie and a Grey Tedburie, each of which is valued at £2 13s. 4d. In fairness to neighbours across the border, the same price is put on the head of a Bay Malmesburie.

There was little clean-cut entertainment in bull-baiting, but as recently as the latter years of the last century the spot in the middle of The Chipping where this barbaric pastime took place was still known and pointed out by townsfolk. Also known to them was an old toast: 'To all our friends round Tetbury bull ring'. And lovers of obscure drama will readily reel off that immortal line from act five of William Sampson's *The Vow-Breaker, Or The Faire Maide Of Clifton*, first, and perhaps last, seen on the stage in 1636: 'He'll keepe more stir with the Hobby Horse than he did with the Pipers at Tedbury Bull-running.' A regular phrase in Court Leet documents in the early years was the order that 'no bull shall be killed before baited or sold by candlelight', the vigorous exercise of the ordeal apparently having been believed to make the meat more tender. If there was one saving grace about our forefathers' cruelty, however, it lay in the fact that they did not reserve it exclusively for dumb animals. The repair of a pillory and stocks was a recurring preoccupation of the Court Leet throughout the seventeenth and eighteenth centuries, and the need to mend the whipping post is noted as late as 1796. As for the ducking stool, the street name Gumstool Hill tells us all we need to know about where that was operated, in a pond at the foot of the steep hill on or around the cattle market pens. The punishment was originally aimed at swindling traders, light measures and faulty wares being one of the banes of the markets. But after a time it turned into the institutionalized bullying of old women regarded as scolds, who would be wheeled into the middle of the pond before being tipped into its filthy depths and hauled out with ropes. It seems that there was little chance of drowning by this process, but it is not hard to believe that the humiliation was so great that some of the victims must surely have wished for such a fate.

CHAPTER SEVEN

Stout Memories

One factor that helped to keep the public house numbers buoyant through much of Victoria's reign was a proliferation of breweries. Stemming from the malting industry of the 1700s, three of them lasted into the present century, the last finally giving way in the 1930s. There were three families involved: the Cooks, the Warns and the Witchells, all of whom set up in business in the early nineteenth century, though the latter two already had well established malt-houses. The striking old brewery building at the corner of Hampton Street and New Church Street, which once served as a wool warehouse, was the Cook's business before it was taken over by the Stroud Brewery in 1913. The Stroud Brewery was later merged into Whitbread's, and so *ad infinitum*. . . . At very much the same time as the Cook's demise, the Warns took over Witchell's Dolphin Brewery, perhaps no great surprise as both were next door neighbours in Church Street. But both moves signalled the same message: the day of the very small independent brewer was over, just as these businesses in their time had put an end to inns making their own beer. By the 1930s this was another Tetbury industry that was strictly for the history books, with Warn's Celebrated Oatmeal Stout and the like no more than a fond memory.

Apart from the not inconsiderable input of the local shopkeepers, building and stone quarrying and stoneware manufacturing have been other industries that have served Tetbury well in living memory, the former particularly so. The firm of Holborow and Sons started as plumbers in 1815, stayed comfortably employed for more than a century after that, and then took flight as builders of housing estates in the inter-war years and particularly the late 1940s, when their payroll went up towards 500. Later ventures into civil engineering were not so successful, but it was nevertheless a considerable shock when the company that had seemingly accounted for almost the entire male workforce of Tetbury in the immediate post-war years ceased to trade. Since there was almost full employment at the time, not least in the building trade, the loss of the Holborow firm did not hit the community as severely as one might expect when a major employer goes under. But it was, nevertheless, a bitter blow, and there are still elderly men in the town who will tell you how the company could have been saved, if only . . .

Watching Holborow's float at the carnival. The town's major employers always put on a good show

Tetbury was equally luckless with the railway. Though a track was first mooted in 1839, linking the town with Stroud, Nailsworth, Avening and Malmesbury, it was another fifty years before the first train steamed in. This delay was particularly hard to take during the 1870s, when the agricultural depression hit communities with poor communications all the more severely. There were several reasons for the hold-up. One was confusion over the gauge to which the tracks might be laid; Tetbury was on the very fringes of GWR territory, and while the rest of the country was happily laying its lines at the standard gauge of 4 ft 8½ in, God's Wonderful Railway still believed that just over seven feet was the measure laid down on tablets of stone. Brunel certainly thought that, and so far as his employees were concerned, his words carried all the force of holy writ.

The other fly in the ointment was Robert Gordon of Kemble House, who owned the vital plot of land on which the Tetbury branch would meet the main line between Swindon and Gloucester. Work on the track from Swindon to Cirencester via Kemble was complete by May 1841, from Kemble to Gloucester by May 1845, and this was rapid progress; 1841, after all, was only a dozen years after Stephenson's Rocket. But Robert Gordon was implacably jealous of the privacy of his land, being one of those early

Goods train at Tetbury station, 1950s

The station, *c.* 1910

Victorian country gentlemen who did not readily accept as a good thing the concept of carriage loads of total strangers being hauled through the heart of their estates by great clanking engines snorting steam and soot. One manifestation of this reluctance of his was the 415-yd Kemble tunnel just east of the station, a feature of the trip to London that still delights little children to this day; the Duke of Beaufort had a similar idea to keep prying eyes off his fields a little further south, at Badminton.

Another of Gordon's ploys was to refuse to let a public station be built on his estate, and though there was a platform at Kemble from the start, it was not until 1872 that the name first appeared on timetables. The first station there worthy of the name opened in 1882, after a railway company director had been stranded for two hours with the 'common herd' in a draughty shed on the Gordons' private platform. Negotiations then began in earnest with Miss Anna Gordon, who eventually relented – so long as the new depot had no refreshment room, and definitely no alcohol. This situation did not change until 1948, when the estate changed hands and a pub was opened nearby.

The GWR had a cunning way with the problem of serving communities it wished to reach but couldn't. It simply built a halt on the line at as convenient a point as possible, which in most cases meant beside some country lane in the middle of nowhere, and put up a signpost proclaiming the name of the wished-for town with the addition of the tell-tale word 'Road'. 'Tetbury Road' was the first spot on which the railway could set a platform to the west of Gordon's estate, and at seven miles distant from the town, it was a classic of the 'Road' tradition. There was even a pub which bore various railway-orientated names until 1963, when the station, renamed Coates since 1906, fell victim to the Beeching axe. It is now known as the Thames Head, being close to one of the claimed sources of the river. Most veterans of GWR travel will have a 'Road' tale to tell, of tipping out of the train expecting to step straight into the town square and instead finding themselves discussing life with two cows and a pheasant. Unhappily, the tradition survives to this day; when travelling Intercity, shun the appendage 'Parkway' with all the vigour of one who has better things to do with a ten pound note than give it away to a cabbie.

Parliamentary approval for the Tetbury branch came in March 1887, with £10,000 granted towards the cost of the seven miles and seventeen chains of line. The first sod was cut in the October, and some £57,000 later, on 2 December 1889, the great day of the opening dawned. Thousands turned out. There were heartfelt banners everywhere: 'May Agriculture Thrive'; 'May Our Trade Flourish'; 'Prosperity To The Trade Of Tetbury'; 'Bright Days Ahead'. Though there were two earlier trains that day, the official one was the 2.20 p.m., arriving back from Kemble at 3.19, and there were grand

'May Agriculture Thrive': triumphal arch at the opening of the railway, 1889

parades on each occasion. Some 200 guests and 390 paying customers travelled that first day, receiving an equally warm reception at the other end of the line; but beyond all the hullabaloo, traders looked forward seriously to a new era of communications, and farmers to the opening of a regular cattle market as a direct result of the rail link with the outer world. These developments came to pass, though not as spectacularly as most would have hoped; who, after all, was to know on that day of banners and marching bands that the great age of steam had already reached its peak?

Most country branch line locomotives had their pet names. They were usually squat and plump little tank engines that inspired affection and condescension in equal measures, and some lovable but slightly comical farm animal usually fitted the bill. In some places it was the *Pig*. In Tetbury it was the *Donkey*, and historian Sid Mosdell says that only once in its long years did it fail to complete its task, when the snow lay deep. It lasted until 1959, when diesel railcars were introduced. These proved quite popular in some parts of the Cotswolds, and are still mourned in the Golden Valley east of Stroud; but they were shunned at Tetbury, to the extent that many of their eight daily journeys would be completely devoid of passengers, and it was a surprise to some that Dr Beeching stayed his axe until as late as 4 April 1964. Ted Prince recalls the high jinks of those last journeys, the packed carriages, the detonators along the line, the tugs on the emergency cord, the coffin for

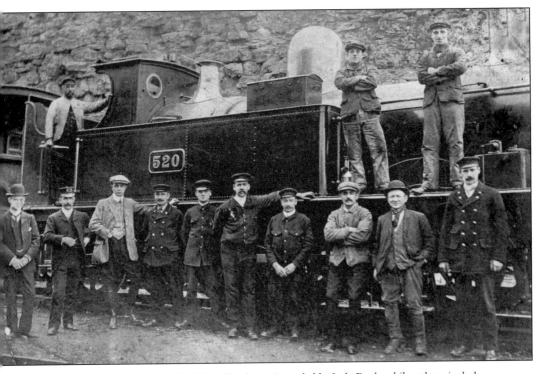

Engine crew and station staff, 1910. The driver is probably Jack Ford, while others include stationmaster Harry Hawker, guard Tommy Curtis, and Charlie Griffiths

Dr Beeching, the beer. He also reflects that if the train had always been as full as it was on the final day of the *Donkey* and the railcars, there would have been no problem in keeping the service open. That is the nub of the matter; for all the crocodile tears, the service was there for the people of Tetbury, and in the end they found they did not need it. Why, indeed, should they have needed it on a regular basis? It gave them an awkward means of getting to Cirencester, a huge dog's hind-leg of a route to Stroud and no way at all to such close neighbours as Malmesbury, Nailsworth and Dursley. If a southbound line had been laid to Bristol via Chipping Sodbury and opened forty years earlier than 1889, Tetbury might today be a very different place, for better or very probably worse. But the fact is that its tasting of the railway age came too little and too late; it is also the case that the few relics of those days of steam still to be seen at the bottom of Silver Street and Gumstool Hill – none of them much more than a hundred years old and some a great deal less – seem more of an anachronism today than all the handiwork of the Stuart and Tudor builders just up the road in town.

In terms of home casualties, Tetbury fared well in the Second World War.

There is a well-loved old tale about the only fatality through bombing being farmer Tom Rich's cow Moonlight, a yarn given an added twist by the fact that so far as can be ascertained, no German bombers flew over Britain on that particular night. The only conclusion to be drawn is that poor old Moonlight was even more luckless than she thought she was, the victim of what is now misnamed friendly fire. It was certainly not unknown for Allied bombers in difficulty to discharge their loads over what their pilots took to be open country, and all over southern England scores of Daisies and Buttercups suffered Moonlight's fate.

That, of course, was by no means the end of it. The town's war memorial – tucked away, rather surprisingly, in St Saviour's churchyard – lists thirty-four men killed in action during the 1939–45 conflict; but over and above this, the hostilities stirred the town more than any other single event this century, and brought German, Italian, American and Polish accents to places where a few years earlier the speech of a Geordie or Yorkshireman would have turned heads. Troops and airmen, both Allied and enemy prisoners, were stationed at camps and airfields throughout the south Cotswolds with the Americans, in particular, making their mark as they did on so many small communities in Europe. The chewing gum, the nylon stockings, the jitterbug records . . .

A plaque is unveiled in 1983 to mark the US Army's Normandy Landings preparations at the Malt House during the Second World War

This was one social revolution in which Tetbury felt at the forefront. It was the first time that had happened in living memory, and to some townsfolk, at least, it felt good. 'The war shook the place up', older residents say. 'It was never the same again.' Whether the change was for good or evil depends on with whom you are talking.

Apart from the lads pouring in from RAF Kemble, Leighterton and elsewhere, there was a strong military presence in the heart of town. In an old malt-house at the top of The Chipping steps, as traditional a corner of the world as any in Britain, members of the 654 United States Topographical Battalion put together a huge model of Omaha Beach to aid their generals to plot the Normandy landings. Not very many people in town knew about that at the time, since the project was as top secret as might be imagined. But there was certainly no mistaking the Town Hall's military footing; it was requisitioned by the War Office for the first few months of hostilities, but from the summer of 1940 it served as a servicemen's canteen, with ARPs given a base in the old fire station and the Home Guard holding a brief to man the entire building should German forces invade. There were the usual morale-boosting drives for aluminium saucepans, savings and food production through allotments, and one way and another, the town centre buzzed like rarely before. With a forces canteen in their midst, the pubs did not do so badly either. The White Hart was a particular favourite, just as it had been for Anzac airmen from Leighterton during the First World War.

The Chipping Steps, a scene of enduring charm

If Tetbury grew into the twentieth century during the Second World War, it has certainly done some further growing since. Private housing estates spread out to the north, many of their roads echoing great names and places in the town's history – Longtree Close, Romney Road, Talboys Walk, Berkeley Way. The northern estates are also the site of Sir William Romney's Community School, at the end of Lowfield Road. It is pleasant that the school's name should commemorate the benefactor whose highly significant will of 1611 included provision for an annual thirteen pounds 'for a schoolmaster to teach the town and parish gratis', but it would be a mistake to suppose that this lively place is in any way a direct descendant of that first great step towards free education. The truth is that the Feoffees fouled up Tetbury Grammar School as conclusively as they did almost everything else they set eyes on in the eighteenth century, to the extent that by 1800 this once proud institution was forced to close.

Boys of the old school: a Tetbury Grammar School cricket team

The town went into the twentieth century with four private secondary schools, three of them for boys, but the upsurge of appetite for social justice after the First World War led to a public meeting to revive the old Grammar, and the fruition of that resolution in 1921. The chosen property was The Ferns, another of those Long Street houses with deceptive amounts of space to the rear, and there the school stayed until its move to Lowfield Road in 1969. There had, however, been a major change in the intervening years, for after the 1944 Education Act, which brought about the abolition of fees, the county education committee drew up a plan for a secondary modern school in Tetbury in which the Grammar School played no part. To save the situation the headmaster, R.J. Woodward, drew up a counter-proposal, and in 1952 a secondary modern stream was introduced alongside the Grammar, with roughly 160 pupils in each. Two years later, with this early English experiment in community education proving to be well worth pursuing, it was clear that the Grammar School label, though pleasing the traditionalists, was no longer tenable. All was not lost for those with a sense of history, however, for when Mr Woodward came up with a new name, it was one that harked back to the birth of free education in the town.

The out-of-town industrial estates off Hampton Street, London Road and Cirencester Road are not collectively bursting at the seams, but they provide work in spheres as diverse as the animal feeds one might expect to be produced in a small country town to specialist products at the cutting edge of microchip technology. Plenty of workers still commute from town daily – but it is by no means one-way traffic at eight-thirty in the morning and six at night, for now people from a wider area than ever before regard Tetbury as their place of employment. A town of antique shops? It certainly is, with a score of them, and 1993 saw a resurgence of outlets in Long Street after a couple of years in the recessionary doldrums. But a town only of antiques? Not by a long way, for the community has learned the lesson of over-dependence on a single trade the hard way, and it will not make the same mistakes again.

Bibliography

Atkyns, Sir Robert: *The Ancient and Present State of Glostershire* (1712).

Gloucestershire Notes and Queries (multiple entries).

A Guide to Tetbury (Tetbury Chamber of Commerce, *c.* 1980).

Hodgson, Eric: *A History of Tetbury* (Alan Sutton, 1978); *Tetbury: a Cotswold Gem* (Tetbury Civic Society, 1979).

Lee, Revd Alfred: *The History of the Town and Parish of Tetbury* (1857).

Massingham, H.J.: *Cotswold Country* (Batsford, 1937).

Mosdell, S.G.: *Take a Walk around Tetbury* (Mosdell, 1976); *Tetbury Market House* (Mosdell, 1976); *Tetbury's Inns and Public Houses* (S.G. & S.R.H. Mosdell); *The Building of Tetbury's Railway* (S.G. & S.R.H. Mosdell, 1977).

Prince, Ted: *Tetbury Till Domesday* (1981).

Tetbury Rural District Guide, 1978.

Ryder, T.A.: *Portrait of Gloucestershire* (Robert Hale, 1966).

Rudder, Samuel: *A New History of Gloucestershire* (1779).

St Mary's Parish Church Guides, 1971 and 1993.

Sutton, Alan: *Tetbury, Nailsworth and Minchinhampton in Old Photographs* (Alan Sutton, 1988); Alan Sutton and John Hudson: *Cotswold Images* (Alan Sutton, 1988).

Verey, David: Gloucestershire, The Cotswolds, from *The Buildings Of England*, ed. Pevsner (Penguin, 1970).

The Victoria History of the County of Gloucester, Volume XI (for University of London Institute of Historical Research by Oxford University Press, 1976).

Wantner, Abel: *History of Gloucestershire* (1714).

Woodman, Marian: *Cotswolds to Calais* (Corinium Museum, 1978).

Index

Agreement, Tetbury, 34
Aldhelm, Abbot, 6, 40
Alfred the Great, 6
Aluricus, 10
Angel Inn, 63, 68
Anne, Queen, 15
Antique shops, 58, 83
Atkyns, Sir Robert, 12, 24, 44, 46, 47, 48, 50
Austen, Jane, 60
Avening, 75
Avon, River, 5

Badminton, 77
Baker, John, 29
Baptists, 57
Barton Abbots, 44
Bath, 6, 15
Bath Bridge, *5, 6*
Baxter, E.N., 7, *10*
Beaufort Hunt and family, 62, 64, 77
Beeching, Dr, 78, 79
Bendall's carriers, 67
Berkeley family, 16, 20, 29, 30
Berkeley Way, 82
Beverston Castle, 13, 14, *14*, 15, 60
Bliss, John, 34
Boot Inn, 68
Box, Richard, 30
Bridgeman, John, 29
Brighton, 17
Bristol, 5, 14, 15, 16, 19, 20, 79
Bristow, Malcolm, *6*
Brownlow, Curate, *49*
Bull-baiting, 73
Butler and Son, 32

Camden's *Britannia*, 11
Carnival, *3, 64, 66, 75*
Cary, Horatio, 14
Castle, 11
Catherine Wheel Inn, 68
Cattle Market, *72*

Chalford, 67
Chapman, Toby, 30
Charles I, 14, 15, 70
Charles II, 15
Charles, Prince of Wales, 15, 53
Charlton, 8
Chavenage, 14
Chipping, The, 24, 32, 37, 42, *46, 56, 57,* 67, 73
Chipping Campden, 19, 36
Chipping Sodbury, 79
Chipping Steps, *33, 60, 81,* 81
Chipping Street, 37
Church Street, *16,* 30, 38, 40, 51, *58, 59,* 59, *61*
Cirencester, 5, 8, 16, 18, 55, 65, 79
Cirencester Road, 83
Clark's Stationers, *16, 58*
Close Hotel, 43, 44, 64–6
Coggan, Lord, 53
Congregational church, *56,* 57
Cook family, 74
Cot's Great Room, 63
Cottage Hospital, 31
Court Leet, 60, 73
Coxwell, Nathaniel, 29
Cromwell, Oliver, 14
Crown Inn, *15,* 69
Cuckold's Knapp, 54
Cutwell Hill, *13*

Daukes, S.W., 55, 56, 57
de Breuse, William and family, 12, 20, 21, 26, 47
de Lurci, Roger, 10, 11, 20
de Prewes, Simon, 46
de St Valery family, *9,* 20, 46
Dolphin Brewery, 74
Dolphin Inn, 68
Domesday Book, 8, 10, 20, 46
Doughton, 8, 15
Doughton Manor, *9,* 30
Dryden, John, 40
Ducking stool, 73

Dunwallo, Malmutius, 11
Dursley, 36, 79

East India Company, 26
Edward I, 15
Edward the Confessor, 10
Eight Bells Hotel, 68
Elmestree, 8
Elmestree House, *9*
Estcourt, 30, *42*, *43*, *44*, 44, 65
Estcourt, Sir Thomas and family, *11*
Ethelred, King of Mercia, 6, 8, 40
Ethelred the Unready, 6
Ethelred I, King of Wessex, 6
Eynsham, Abbey, 46

Fairford, 19
Fair Maide Of Clifton, 73
Feoffees, 16, *17*, 22, 26–35, 37, 38, 41, 49, 82
Foss Way, 8, 11, 16
Foster, John, 50
Frampton, Revd John, 56

Gastrell, John and family, 30, 44, 48
George II, 49
Gibbs, James, 49
Gloucester, 10, 14, 15, 18, 22, 25, 75
Godwin, Earl, 10
Goldings carriers, 67
Gordon family, 75, 77
Goulding, Douglas, *17*
Grammar School, 82–3
Green, The, 8, *15*, 57, 71
Gumstool Hill, *15*, 70, *71*, 72, 73, 79
Guthlac, Saint, 8

Haberdashers' Company, 26
Hackett or Hickett Court, 44
Hamilton-Yatman, W., 53–4
Hampton Street, *1*, 74, 83
Harold, King, 10
Hazleton, 45
Henry VIII, 11
Hexham, John, 22
Highgrove, 15, 30, 53–4, 70
Hiorn, Francis, 51, 53
Hodges, Thomas, 29
Holborow and Sons, 74, *75*
Holford, R.S., 62
Horton, 12
Horwood, Revd T.G., 53
Hotels and inns, 58–69
Hudson Bay, 27
Hudson, Henry, 27

Huntley, Sir George, 29
Hussey's plumbers, *71*
Hwicce, 5

Ina, King of Wessex, 8

Jackaments Bottom, 8
James I, 29
James II, 15
John, King, 20
Jolly Butchers, *62*, 68
Jones, Charlie, *19*, *35*
Joseph, Maxwell, 64

Keble, John, 56
Kemble, 8, 75, 77, 81
Kimber, Brian, *24*
King and Queen Inn, 66
Kingswood, 42, 45, 46

Lacock, 11
Lamb, E.T., *28*, *48*
Lamb Inn, 66
Lansdown, Thomas S., 57
Lasborough, *11*
Latter-day Saints, 57
Lee, Revd Alfred, 46, 47, 55, 58
Leighterton, 81
Leland, John, 11
Llewellyn, Venerable W.S., 53
London, 26, 77
London Road, *40*, 70, 83
Long Newnton, 8
Long Street, *16*, *36*, 38, *40*, 40, *58*, 64, *65*, 66, 83
Longtree, 10
Longtree Close, 82
Lowder, Father Charles, 56
Lowfield Road, 82, 83

Macbeth, 10
Magdalen Meadow spring, 24, *24*
Malmesbury, 6, 11, 12, 15, 57, 73, 75, 79
Malt House, *80*, 81
Market House or Town Hall, 6, *17*, 22, 25, 35, 36–41, 54, 59, 60, *62*, 68, 81
Market Place, 37, *38*, 59, 62, 67, *68*
Massey, Colonel, 14, 15
Massingham, H.J., 39
Matilda, Queen, 13, 45
Merchant Venturers' Company, 26
Mercia, 5, 6
Methodists, 57
Midland Railway, 41, 66
Minchinhampton, 67

Monasteries, 42–6
Moonlight the cow, 80
Morrison-Bell, Colonel E.F., 66
Mosdell, Sid, *17*, 39, 67, 78
Mowbray family, 12
Munday, Wallace, *28*

Nailsworth, 66, 75
New Church Street, 54, 74
New Palace Cinema, 63
Northanger Abbey, 60
North Hayes, 8
Northleach, 19
North Nibley, 29

Oglethorpe, Colonel, 14, 15
Oldham, John, 40
Old Post Office Stores, *65*
Ormonde, Duke of, 66
Ormond's Head or Gentle Gardener, 39, *41*, 66, 68
Oxford, 5, 49, 56

Paul family, *9*, 65
Perrett family, 63
Population, 3, 8, 10
Price, Dennis, *12*
Prince and Princess Inn, 63, 67, *68*
Prince of Wales Inn, 70, *70*
Prince, Ted, 8, 40, 78
Princess Ju Ju, *52*
Priory, The, 42, 44, 45
Priory Inn, 70
Prouts Stores, *65*

Races, Tetbury, 70
Railway and station, *51*, 63, 67, *68*, 75–9, *76*, 78, *79*
Rich, Tom, 80
Robert of Gloucester, 13
Roman Catholics, 57
Romans, 6, 11
Romney Road, 82
Romney, Sir William, 26–9, 30, 40, 48, 82
Royal Oak, *2*, *19*, *35*
Rudder, Samuel, 12, 46
Rudolph of Germany, 8

Sadler family, *9*
Saintbury, 12
St Mary's parish church, 6, 12, 19, 46–54, *54*
St Michael's church, 57
St Saviour's church, *54*, 54–6, 80
Sampson, William, 73
Sandes, Sir William, 29

Sandwich, 19
Saunders, Samuel, 34
Savage, Francis, 34, 65
Savage, John, 48
Scots, 16
Sealey, William, 60
Seede family, 65
Shakespeare, William, 10
Sherwood, Revd Michael, 53
Silver Street, *15*, 79
Sir William Romney's Community School, 82, 83
Siward, Earl of Northumberland, 10
Smyth, John, 29, 30, 32
Soldier Inn, 68
Southampton, 19
Stedwell, Robert, 29
Stephen, King, 13, 45
Stroud, 14, 24, 74, 75, 78
Swindon, 75

Talbot Hotel, 68, *69*
Talboys, Richard and family, *9*, 30
Tetbury *Donkey*, 78, 79
Tetbury Road station, 77
Tetta, 6, 8, 42
Thames and Severn Canal, 24
Thames Head Hotel, 77
Thirteen, 22, 28, 30, 34, 41
Three Cups Hotel, *59*, 59–60, 63
Tintern Abbey, 42, 45
Titherington, 12
Town Hall *see* Market House
Transport Company, Tetbury, 67
Trouble House, *63*
Tugwell, Richard, 71

United Reformed church, 57
Upton, 8, 10

Verey, David, 37, 42, 51
Vulliamy, Lewis, 62

Wantner, Abel, 24
Warn family, *21*, 74
Warren or Common, 35
Webb, Edwin, *69*
Wessex, 5, 6, 8
Westonbirt, 62
Weston-super-Mare, *47*
West Saxons, 5
West Street, 70
White Hart or Snooty Fox Hotel, 62–4, 67, 81
White Lion Hotel, 63
Whittington, Richard, 26

Wight, Revd John, 48, 50, 51
Wilton Bridge, 24
Wimborne, Dorset, 8
Winchcombe, 18
Witchell family, *59*, 60, 74
Wood, John, elder and younger, 2
Woodstock, 15
Woodward, R.J., 83
Woollen trade, 1, 2, 18–25, 58
Woolsack race, 70

Wotton-under-Edge, 36, 42
Wright, F.W., *23*
Wyatt, James, *11*

Acknowledgements and thanks for use of photographs are due to the Ted Prince collection; the collection of Malcolm and Jill Bristow, which includes F.N. Baxter's photographic plates; and the Bristol United Press, publishers of the *Western Daily Press* and *Bristol Evening Post*.